Pigs, Piglets, and Porkers

Pigs, Piglets, and Porkers

Alison Wormleighton

Chilton Book Company
Radnor, Pennsylvania

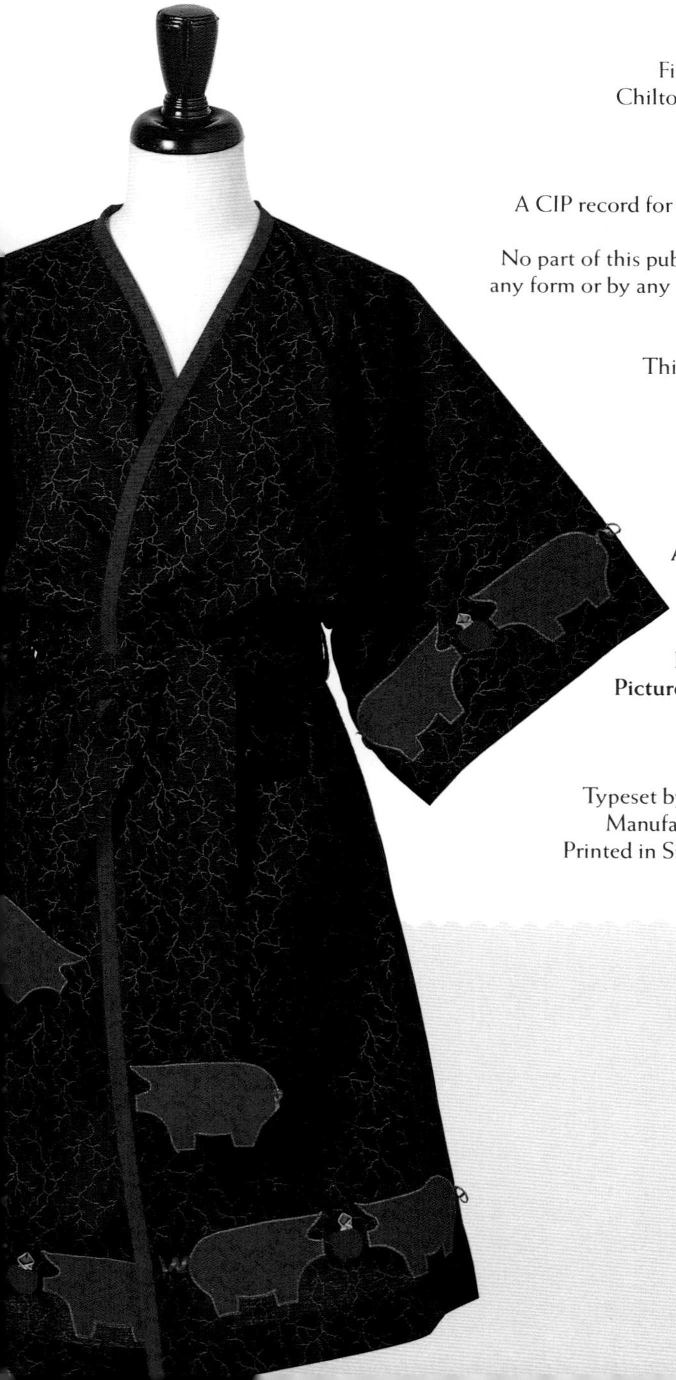

A QUARTO BOOK

Copyright © 1995 Quarto Inc.

ISBN 0-8019-8730-X

A CIP record for this book is available from the Library of Congress.

This book was designed and produced by
Quarto Inc.
The Old Brewery
6 Blundell Street
London N7 9BH

Senior editor Sally MacEachern
Art editors Julie Francis, Liz Brown
Designer Julie Francis
Illustrator Elsa Godfrey
Photographer Paul Forrester
Picture researcher Susannah Jayes
Picture research manager Giulia Hetherington
Art director Moira Clinch
Editorial director Mark Dartford

Typeset by Central Southern Typesetters, Eastbourne
Manufactured in Singapore by Eray Scan Pte Ltd
Printed in Singapore by Star Standard Industries (Pte) Ltd

CONTENTS

INTRODUCING PIGS

Pigs are among the best-loved of all animals, and it is easy to see why. As the novelist G. K. Chesterton explained, "Pigs are very beautiful animals . . . There is no point of view from which a really corpulent pig is not full of sumptuous and satisfying curves."

In perfect counterpoint to the pig's lovely rotund shape are its dainty hoofs (called trotters only in a culinary context) each with four toes, and the little curly tail.

CHECK MATES
pages 42–3

I<small>RRESISTIBLE</small>

Apart from its aesthetic virtues, and of course its culinary value, the pig has many other endearing qualities. It is a clean animal and is also intelligent, as George Orwell acknowledged in "Animal Farm" when he wrote, "The work of teaching and organizing fell naturally upon the pigs, who were generally recognized as being the cleverest of animals."

Even the pig's legendary greed is to most people a likable trait, since we recognize something of ourselves in the pig's inclinations, if not its table manners. Yet the pig's most appealing feature has to be its face. Who can resist the floppy ears, the upturned nose, and the indisputable smile?

PIGGIES IN THE MIDDLE
pages 36–9

PREPARE TO
PIG OUT
pages 88–91

THIS LITTLE PIGGY
pages 72–3

PEARLS BEFORE SWINE
pages 60–3

ANCESTRY

In parts of Europe, wild pigs still forage on the forest floor for their favorite foods: truffles, acorns, beech nuts, roots. America's only wild pigs are the razorback hogs found in Southern swampland. Domesticated pigs, however, are descended from Asiatic wild pigs. Those that are reared intensively are fed a special diet, while others, living in sties in small enclosures, or in wooden kuts in fields, feed on roots, worms, and household scraps. Sometimes they are kept as pets, following their owners around as companionably as dogs.

PIGS OF YOUR OWN

Despite their obvious attractions, you may decide that a pig is just not the pet for you. Yet it is perfectly possible to enjoy that friendly face and podgy shape without going the whole hog and investing in a pig pen. With "Pigs, Piglets, and Porkers" you can make your own collection of personable pigs, ranging from the highly practical to the purely decorative.

You can tailor the style (stylized, realistic, humorous) to the nature of the project, the person who will use it, the materials it is made from, or the techniques it involves. With step-by-step directions, diagrams, and patterns, plus basic techniques and stitches at the back of the book, you can't go wrong — even if you've always thought you were ham-fisted.

PIGS ON THE TABLE
pages 46–9

DECORATIVE PIGS

I never could imagine why pigs should not be kept as pets. To begin with, pigs are very beautiful animals. Those who think otherwise are those who do not look at anything with their own eyes, but only through other people's eyeglasses.

G. K. Chesterton, *The Uses of Diversity*

This pretty hanging decoration consists of stuffed

HAMSTRUNG

fabric pigs linked together by beads threaded onto embroidery thread (an altogether nicer type of pork links!). Choose coordinating small-scale prints for a patchwork effect, and echo the colors with the beads. Here, delicate floral prints, mainly in pastel tones, were used, but bright primary-colored prints such as French provincial or Indian fabrics would look equally effective. The curly tails are made by binding embroidery floss around pipe cleaners.

MATERIALS

Finished length 33 inches

- Six 12 x 8 inch pieces of cotton fabric, each in a different small print
- Sewing thread to match
- Kapok stuffing
- Pipe cleaners
- Pink embroidery floss
- 12 sequins
- 62 beads
- Bell

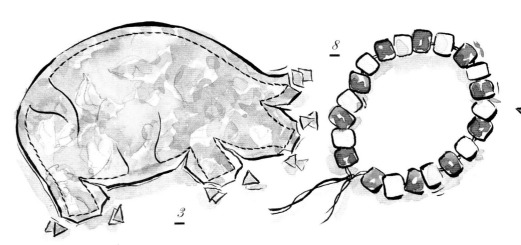

CUTTING OUT

1 Using the pattern on page 113, cut out two pig shapes from each of the six fabric pieces, so that in each pair one is the mirror image of the other.

MAKING THE PIGS

2 Place a pair of pig shapes with right sides together and stitch all around the edge, taking a ⅜ inch seam, and pivoting at corners. Leave a 1¼ inch gap on the belly and a ¼ inch gap where the tail will go. Repeat for the other five pairs of pig shapes.

3 Trim the seams, clip into the inner corners, and clip across the outer corners, then turn the pigs right sides out.

4 Stuff each pig with kapok, inserting it through the hole in the belly until the pig is a nice, fat, rounded shape. Be sure to push the kapok right down inside the snout, ears, and feet. Slipstitch the gap in the belly closed.

5 Cut six 2¼ inch lengths of pipe cleaner. Bind each with pink embroidery floss, knotting the floss at the start and finish, to prevent it from unraveling.

6 Insert one end into the small gap for the tail. Sew it in place, and twist the tail to form a curl. Repeat for the other five pigs.

7 For the eyes of each pig, sew a sequin onto each side of the head.

STRINGING THE PIGS TOGETHER

8 Cut a 78 inch length of embroidery floss and thread it onto a needle so you have a double length. Knot the ends. Thread 21 beads onto the floss, alternating colors, then knot the beaded part into a loop.

9 Take the needle and floss through the middle of one pig, from the center of the back to the center of the belly, drawing the floss through so that the bead loop is above its back.

10 Thread eight more beads onto the embroidery floss, again alternating colors. Thread the needle through the next pig in the same way as before. Continue until all the pigs are linked together, with eight beads between them.

11 Under the belly of the bottom pig, thread a bead and a bell onto the embroidery floss, then sew the end securely in place. Hang from the beaded loop.

PIG POCKETS

With nine roomy pockets, this colorful holdall is just the thing to hang in the family room, hall, or playroom. It will happily swallow up all those bits and pieces that are left around to clutter up the home — yet it is so attractive that you may prefer to use it simply as a wallhanging. Choose fabrics that match the other furnishings in the room, or that go with your color scheme. (Patchwork suppliers are good sources of small pieces of coordinating fabrics.) Use the background fabric, in this case check gingham, to unify them all.

Finished size 35¾ inches wide x 38½ inches high

MATERIALS

- 2⅛ yards gingham 45 inches wide, for background
- Two 11 inch squares of each of 9 different prints
- Nine 9 inch squares of

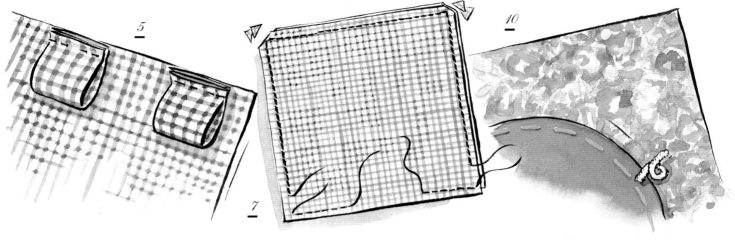

CUTTING OUT

1 From the gingham background fabric, cut two 37 inch squares, and two 5 x 27 inch strips.

2 Using the pattern on page 121, cut out a pig from each of the nine pieces of felt.

MAKING THE BACKGROUND

3 With right sides together and raw edges even, pin the two strips of gingham together along the long edges. Stitch both seams, taking a ⅜ inch seam allowance. Turn right side out. Press.

4 Cut the strip into four equal segments, each measuring 6¾ x 4¼ inches. Fold each segment in half so that the raw edges meet.

5 With raw edges even, pin the folded segments to the top of one gingham square, spacing them equally and allowing a ⅝ inch gap at the side edges of the gingham. Baste them in place.

6 With right sides together and raw edges even, lay the other gingham square on top, sandwiching the hanging loops in between the layers.

7 Pin and stitch around all four edges, taking a ⅝ inch seam. Leave an opening in the base for turning through and an opening in the bottom 1¼ inches of each side seam. (The bottom dowel will be slotted through here later.) Trim off the top corners and turn right side out. Press. Slipstitch the opening in the base.

MAKING THE POCKETS

8 With right sides together and raw edges even, join the matching print squares to each other on all four sides, taking a ⅜ inch seam and leaving an opening for turning through. Trim corners and turn right side out. Press. Slipstitch the opening in each.

9 Center a felt pig on each pocket, and sew it on using the embroidery floss (all six strands) and long running stitches. Note that the pig in the middle is sewn on in reverse.

10 Make each tail by curling a short length of pipe cleaner around a pencil, then sew one onto each pig. Sew on buttons for eyes.

11 Position the pockets on the background, leaving equal gaps between them and around the edges. Baste in place, then stitch down one side, along the bottom, and up the other side of each pocket. At the beginning and end, reinforce the stitching with a small triangle.

12 Slot a dowel through the hanging loops and another through the base. Attach a cord to the ends of the top dowel, for hanging.

- *felt in assorted colors*
- *Sewing thread to match background and print fabrics, and in white*
- *Stranded embroidery floss in assorted colors*
- *Pipe cleaners*
- *Nine small buttons, for the pigs' eyes*
- *Two 39 inch lengths of ¼ inch dowel*
- *Cord, for hanging*

Let Sleeping Pigs Lie

What could be more peaceful than this contented pair? Reclining gracefully across the pillow, they are the picture of porcine bliss. The bold, simple outline of the appliquéd design looks best in a plain but elegant fabric such as the silk dupion used here. Quilting with a decorative machine satin stitch in a deeper tone of pink emphasizes the outline subtly but effectively. Because the pillow form cannot be removed from the cover (and because silk fabric has been used), this pillow should only be dry-cleaned. It is therefore advisable to give these pigs pride of place in a bedroom.

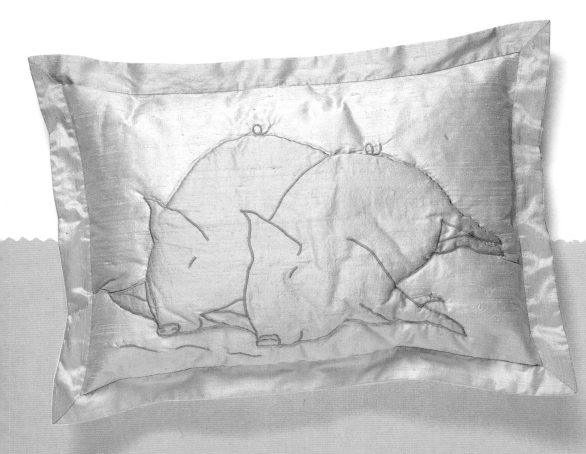

Finished size, including flange, 23¾ x 18¾ inches.

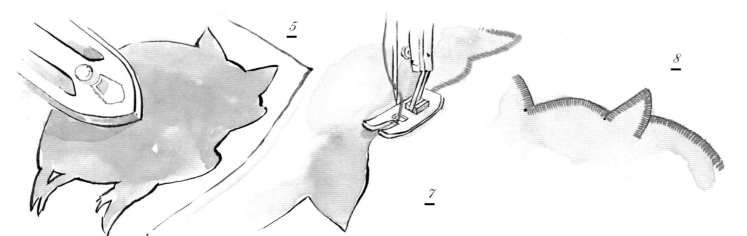

CUTTING OUT

1 From the beige fabric, cut a 20 x 15 inch piece for the front and a 25 x 20 inch piece for the back.

2 From the pink fabric, cut an 18 x 12 inch piece for the pigs.

3 From the beige fabric, cut two 3 x 20 inch strips and two 3 x 25 inch strips for the flanged border.

APPLIQUÉ

4 Trace the pattern on page 114 and transfer the outline onto fusible web. (Do not transfer the features or cut it out at this stage.)

5 Place the fusible web, adhesive-side downward, on the wrong side of the pink fabric. Following the manufacturer's directions, use a dry iron to iron the fusible web onto the fabric. Carefully cut out around the outer edge of the design.

6 Remove the backing of the fusible web and place the pigs on the right side of the pillow front, adhesive side down, positioning them centrally. Press carefully over the whole design area with a hot, dry iron. Do not use a damp cloth as it may mark the silk. Leave to cool. (The adhesion of the fusible web will not be affected by dry-cleaning.)

DECORATIVE STITCHING

7 Using the browny-pink thread and a short, narrow machine satin stitch, stitch around the outline to cover the raw edges.

8 When you reach a corner or point, you will need to pivot the needle before continuing. If it is an outer corner, stop the needle on the outside before pivoting. If it is an inner corner, stop the needle on the inside, and then pivot. To work around a tight curve, you will need to stop and pivot frequently; always stop the needle on the narrower side of the curve before pivoting and carrying on.

9 When the stitching is finished, pull the thread ends through to the wrong side, and tie in a knot.

MATERIALS

- 1 yard beige silk dupion 45 inches wide, for background of pillow front and for flanged border and back
- ⅓ yard pink silk dupion 45 inches wide, for pigs
- Sewing thread to match beige fabric, and in deep browny-pink shade, and in green
- Fusible web
- ½ yard of lightweight batting
- 20 x 15 inch pillow form

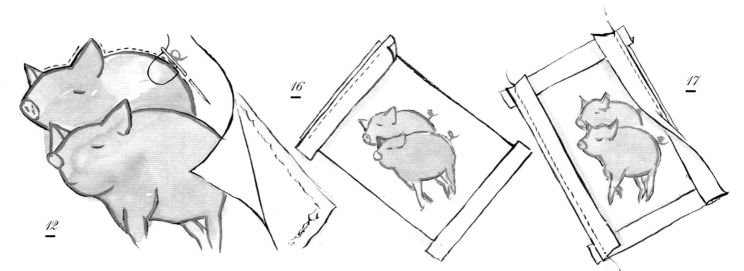

10 Transfer the pigs' features, tails, and any remaining lines of the design onto the main shape, and stitch these in the same way.

11 Make three wavy lines beneath the pigs' snouts, to represent grass, and then machine satin-stitch these lines in the same way too, using green thread.

QUILTING

12 Lay batting on the wrong side of the fabric and baste it in place. Working from the right side and using short, closely spaced running stitches, quilt around the outside of the pig outline. As you get used to quilting, you may be able to pick up several stitches before pushing the needle through each time, which is obviously much quicker than pulling the needle through with each individual stitch.

13 On the wrong side, trim away excess batting from outside the stitching line, but do not trim so close to the stitching that there is a risk of the batting's coming loose.

FLANGED BORDER

14 With right sides together and raw edges even, lay one of the shorter border strips along one side edge of the pillow front. The strip should extend beyond the top and bottom edge of the pillow front by 2½ inches. (When the flanged border is complete, these will all be flush with the edge.)

15 Pin and stitch the border strip to the pillow along the raw edge, taking a ¼ inch seam and stopping the stitching ¼ inch short of the top and bottom edges of the pillow front. Press the border strip to the right side.

16 Repeat steps 14 and 15 for the remaining shorter strip, which goes on the other side edge of the pillow front.

17 Stitch the two longer strips to the top and bottom edges of the pillow front in the same way as for the sides. Again, stop the stitching ¼ inch short of the side edges – in other words, when you reach the seamline of each of the side borders. Press these strips to the right side too.

18 Working from the right side, turn under the bottom corner of one end of the top border strip, making a diagonal fold over the side border strip. Press the fold.

19 Now, working on the wrong side, pin and carefully stitch along the diagonal line you have just pressed, to make a neat, mitered corner.

20 Repeat steps 18 and 19 for the other end of the top border strip.

TIPS

• Using fusible web to secure the design and a machine satin stitch to finish the edges is the quickest and easiest form of appliqué. Fusible web works best on large, simple shapes, as it can be difficult to align the fabric and web when working on small or intricate shapes.

• When quilting, it's important always to catch all the layers with the stitches. Here there are only two layers (pillow front and batting) but often there is a backing

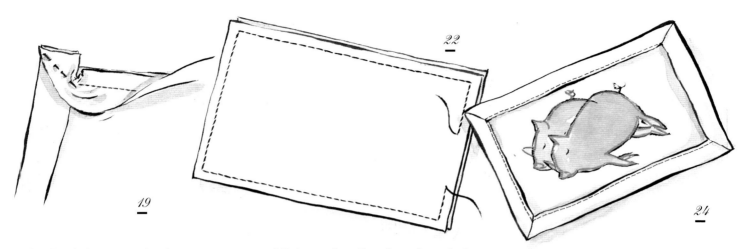

21 Similarly, turn under the top corner of one end of the bottom border strip, making a diagonal fold. Press, then, once again, pin and stitch along the diagonal pressed line from the wrong side. Repeat for the other end of the bottom border strip.

MAKING UP THE PILLOW

22 With right sides together and raw edges even, pin and stitch the pillow back to the pillow front along all edges, leaving an opening for the pillow form on one short side, and taking a ⅝ inch seam.

23 Trim the corners. Turn the pillow cover right side out through the opening, and press.

24 Topstitch through the pillow front and back along the inside edge of the flanged border on three sides, leaving the side with the opening unstitched at this stage.

25 Insert the pillow form through the opening in the side of the cover. Slipstitch the opening closed. Press the stitched edge.

26 Topstitch along the inside edge of this flanged edge to match the other three topstitched edges.

layer as well. It helps to hold your other hand underneath the item, so that you can feel the needle come through with each stitch.

FAIR & SQUARE

Not only do these square herbal pillows have a nice fat pig as the central motif but they also utilize that classic trio — patchwork, appliqué, and embroidery. The techniques complement each other well, resulting in pillows that look delightful as well as smelling sweet. In both, the borders are built up as in log cabin patchwork and the edges/seams are hand-embroidered — yet the different colorways, border designs, and arrangement of stitches, as well as the use of crazy patchwork for one pig, give each pillow its own distinct identity.

Finished size 10 inches square

MATERIALS

For each pillow:

- ½ yard muslin 36 inches wide, for background
- ¼ yard check gingham or plaid cotton fabric 36

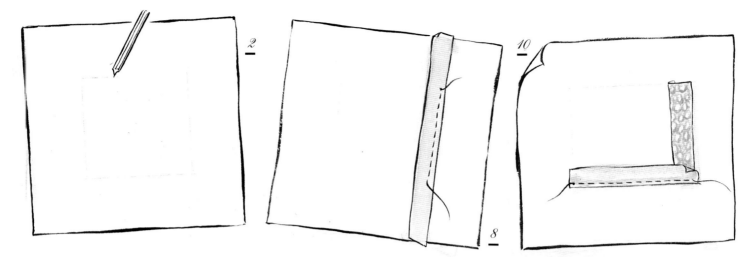

CUTTING OUT AND PREPARATION

1 Cut a 12 inch square from muslin. Fold and press it diagonally in both directions in order to find the center point.

2 Draw a 6½ inch square in the center of the muslin square, measuring 3¼ inches out from the central point to each side to insure that the square is exactly in the center. The corners will be on the diagonal folds.

3 Cut four 12 x 1½ inch strips from muslin.

4 *Plaid pillow only*: Cut a 5 inch square of muslin.

5 *Plaid pillow only*: Using the pattern on page 113, cut out four triangles from the plaid fabric.

6 Cut two 8 x 12 inch pieces of red check gingham (for the red check pillow) or plaid fabric (for the plaid pillow).

7 Using the pattern on page 113, trace the pig motif onto the backing paper of the fusible web. Cut out the pig shape roughly. (It will be cut out exactly at a later stage.)

LOG CABIN PATCHWORK BORDER

8 For the log cabin border, strips of fabric are applied in "rounds" (four strips – one per side) around the central calico square, in clockwise order, with the ends overlapping and the strips getting progressively longer. You can start on any side you like, as long as you start on the same side for each round. The first round consists of patterned fabric strips. With right sides together, place the first strip inside the square, aligning the edge with one side of the square. Pin and stitch from one side of the square to the opposite side, taking a ¼ inch seam.

9 Fold this strip back to its right side, and press. Trim off the surplus fabric at the ends, so that it is flush with the edge of the square.

10 In the same way, apply the next strip to the adjacent edge, positioning it so that it extends all the way to the outside edge of the previous strip, stitching right to that edge.

11 Do the same for two more patterned strips. The first round is now completed.

12 Apply the second round (muslin strips) in the same way, and following the same order, which means starting on the same side as you did for the first round. This time, take ½ inch seams.

inches wide, for pillow back, and for pig on red check pillow

• 12 x 1½ inch strips of four patterned fabrics: two of each (red check pillow) or one of each (plaid pillow)

• Scraps of patterned fabrics, for pig (plaid pillow)

• Fusible web

• Stranded embroidery floss in red and green (red check pillow) or in cream and terracotta (plaid pillow)

• Sewing thread

• Scrap of fine gauzy cotton, for herb sachet

• Dried herbs (see Tips)

• 10 inch pillow form

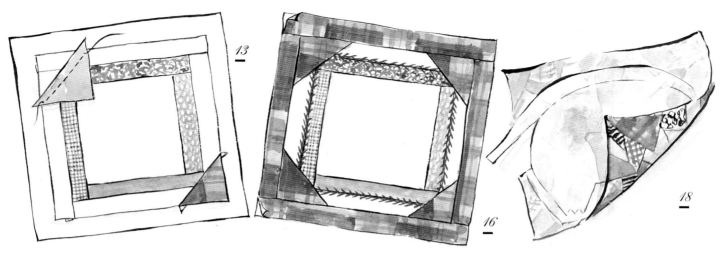

13

16

18

13 *Plaid pillow only*: With right sides together, place one of the plaid triangles across each corner of the log cabin borders. Position each triangle so that when you have stitched across the outer edge taking a ¼ inch seam, the seamline will cross the seamline between the first and second rounds, on both edges. Stitch, and then fold each triangle back to its right side, and press.

14 Now apply the last round, which is four more strips of the patterned fabrics (for the red check pillow) or four strips of the plaid fabric (for the plaid pillow). The positions of the patterned strips for the red check pillow should be different from those of the first round for added contrast. This time, take a ¼ inch seam.

EMBROIDERY

15 *Red check pillow only*: Using three strands of green embroidery floss, work large cross-stitches over the seamlines between the first and second rounds, centering each stitch over the seamline. Then, using two strands of red embroidery floss, work feather stitch between the second and third rounds, once again centering the stitches over the seamlines.

16 *Plaid pillow only*: Using two strands of terracotta embroidery floss, embroider the seam between the first and second rounds in feather stitch.

APPLIQUÉ

17 *Red check pillow only*: Following the manufacturer's directions, iron the pig shape that you cut out of fusible web onto the wrong side of the red check gingham fabric. Cut out around the outline of the pig.

18 *Plaid pillow only*: Following the manufacturer's directions, apply fusible web to the wrong side of the assorted scraps of fabric. Cut out small, irregular shapes, remove the backing paper, and fuse them onto the 5 inch square of muslin. Try to arrange the various fabric pieces so that, though random, the crazy patchwork is balanced in terms of both color and pattern. Continue until the entire piece is covered, with no gaps between shapes. Now iron the fusible web pig shape onto the wrong side of the muslin square containing the applied crazy patchwork. Cut out carefully around the pig outline.

TIPS

● These cross-stitches should not be embroidered immediately next to each other like they would be in counted-thread embroidery; there should be a gap between adjacent stitches. The gingham makes a useful guide for keeping the stitch width and distance between them constant.

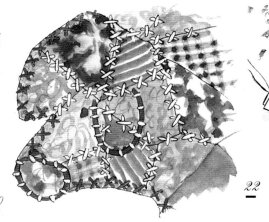

20

25

22

19 Remove the backing paper and fuse the pig onto the pillow front, positioning it in the center of the muslin square.

20 Using two strands of embroidery floss in green (for the red check pillow) or terracotta and cream (for the plaid pillow), work cross-stitch around the outline of the pig (and, on the plaid pillow only, over all the lines of the crazy patchwork). This time, work small crosses, positioning them completely on the pig, rather than trying to center them over the edge.

21 Using two strands of embroidery floss in green couched with red stitches (for the red check pillow) or in terracotta couched with cream stitches (for the plaid pillow), embroider the features of the ear, snout, back leg, and tail.

22 Use the same color (green or terracotta) to embroider a small eye on the pig.

MAKING UP

23 Finish one long side on each of the two fabric rectangles which you cut for the back, by turning under ¼ inch and pressing, and then turning under a further ½ inch. Press and stitch.

24 On the front, trim the muslin backing even with the outer edge of the log cabin border. Pin the two back pieces onto the front piece with right sides together and raw edges even, overlapping the hemmed edges of the back. Pin and stitch around all four edges, taking a ½ inch seam. Trim the corners and turn right side out through the opening in the back. Push out the corners, and press.

25 To make a sachet of herbs, use pinking shears to cut out two 2 inch squares of fine cotton, and stitch them together along three sides, taking a ¼ inch seam. Insert your chosen selection of herbs and then stitch up the remaining side. Tack the herb sachet to the pillow form.

26 Insert the pillow form into the cover through the back opening, so that the sachet is at the front.

● For a stronger-smelling herb pillow, make a fine muslin or gauzy cotton lining the size of the pillow, fill it with dried herbs, then use this instead of a pillow form. Make it in the same way as the sachet, only bigger. To make the herbs less crackly, add a few drops of floral oil.

● The herbs used in a herb pillow, whether in the lining or in a sachet, need to be quite dry and crumbly, but they should not actually be powdery.

HIGGLEDY PIGGLEDY

This pretty pillow shows off appliqué and embroidery skills that look charming and are easy to master. Simple pig shapes in pastel prints are scattered around at random and hand-appliquéd to green linen, the color of a field in springtime. Stylized flowers are embroidered among them for an even more bucolic effect. This type of flanged pillow cover with an overlap closure at the back is stylish and practical, yet also remarkably quick and easy. The size can be adapted to your own requirements, whether larger or smaller.

Finished size 20½ inches square

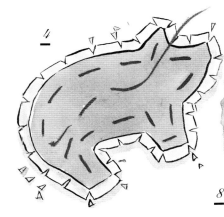

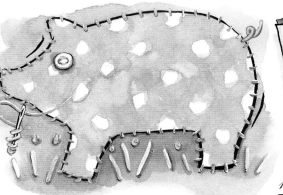

CUTTING OUT

1 From the linen background fabric, cut out a 21¾ inch square for the front, and a 21¾ x 27 inch rectangle for the back. Cut the rectangle in half to form two 21¾ x 13½ inch pieces; this cutting line will be the center edge.

2 Using the patterns on page 118, cut out six pig shapes from the paper.

3 Press the print fabrics with a warm iron, and pin the six paper templates to them. (Some should be pinned on to face in the opposite direction to the others.) Cut around each template, leaving a seam allowance of just over ¼ inch all around.

APPLIQUÉ

4 Using small, sharp embroidery scissors, snip into the seam allowances at tight corners or on curves. Baste the templates to the wrong side of the fabric shapes.

5 For each pig, turn the seam allowance to the wrong side over the template, pressing with an iron as you go. Now take out the basting and remove the templates.

6 Arrange the pigs over the front of the pillow cover, but avoid placing them within about 2½ inches of the edges. Pin in position, making sure the seam allowances are all turned under.

7 Using colored embroidery flosses that will show up against the fabrics, slipstitch or blindstitch the pigs in place all around the folded edge. If the seam allowances pop out in places, use the point of the needle to push them back under.

EMBROIDERY

8 Embroider curly tails on the pigs using backstitch, then embroider grass and flowers using simple straight stitches and French knots. Sew on buttons for eyes.

9 If desired, stitch on ribbon trim. Position it either ¾ inch from the edge (so it will be on the edge of the flange) or 1⅜ inches from the edge (so it will be inside the flange).

MAKING UP THE PILLOW

10 To make the back of the cover, press under ¼ inch and then press under another 1 inch on the center edge of both pieces. Stitch these double hems in place.

11 With right sides together and raw edges even, pin the back pieces to the front piece, with the hemmed edges overlapping in the center. Stitch all around the raw edges, taking a ⅝ inch seam. Turn the cover right side out through the center back opening. Press.

12 To make the flanged edge, topstitch around all four sides, ⅝ inch from the edge. Insert a pillow form through the back opening.

MATERIALS

- 1 yard green linen, 45 inches wide, for the background
- Scraps of 6 different lightweight cottons in small-scale prints
- Sewing thread to match
- Embroidery floss in contrasting colors
- Brown wrapping paper, or good-quality writing paper
- 2⅓ yards ribbon trim (optional)
- Small pearly buttons, for the eyes
- 18 inch pillow form

PIG OF THE BUNCH

This pig serves no practical purpose whatsoever — but when you're covered from head to toe in bunches of beautiful roses, you don't have to be useful. It's enough just to be a source of delight to anyone who gazes upon you. Little children will love cuddling her, but really this is a pig for adults. Her sophisticated chintz covering and well-upholstered shape have suited her to a life of leisure and frivolity; although actually quite robust, she prefers being pampered. Presiding over a pile of pillows on a bed or sofa, a pig like this could start to get delusions of grandeur.

Finished size 14 inches long x 6½ inches wide x 7¾ inches high

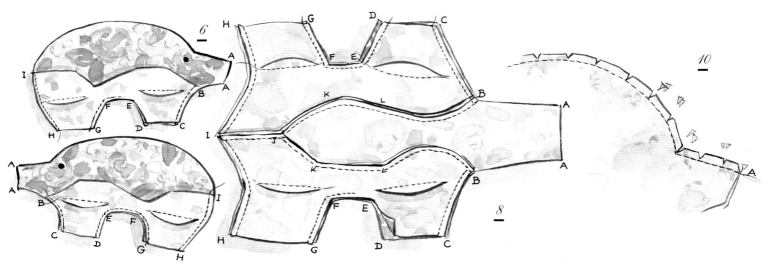

CUTTING OUT

1 Using the patterns on pages 114–15, cut out from chintz two body pieces (one in reverse), one inner underbody piece, two outer underbody pieces (one in reverse), four ear pieces (two in reverse), two tail pieces, a 2¼ inch circle for the snout, and four 2¾ inch circles for the foot pads.

2 From thin cardboard, cut a 1½ inch circle for the snout and four 2 inch circles for the foot pads.

MAKING THE EARS AND EYES

3 With right sides together, join two ear pieces from point M down one side and up the other to point N, taking a ⅛ inch seam. Clip the curves, turn right side out, and press. Turn under the raw edges and slipstitch the opening. Repeat.

4 To insert each eye make a tiny hole as marked on the pattern. Push the stalk through from the right side. Push the washer onto the stalk.

MAKING THE BODY

5 On the wrong side of the outer underbody piece, stitch the darts.

6 With right sides together, pin one outer underbody piece to one body piece, matching points B–I. Stitch from B–C, from F–G and from H–I, taking a ¼ inch seam. Repeat for the other outer underbody and body pieces but stitch from B–C, D–G, and H–I.

7 With right sides together, join the outer underbody pieces from I–J, taking a ¼ inch seam.

8 With right sides together, join the outer and inner underbodies from B–L–K–J on both sides, taking a ¼ inch seam.

9 Stitch the tail pieces together along the dotted line shown on the pattern, with right sides together. Turn right side out and press. Turn the raw edges under and slipstitch, stuffing the tail as you go. Sew onto the body where shown.

10 With the pig still wrong side out, join the body pieces along the top from A–I, making sure the tail is on the inside and taking a ¼ inch seam. Clip into the corner at the start of the snout and the curves.

11 With right sides together, join the inner underbody to the body from A–B on both sides, taking ¼ inch seams.

FINISHING

12 Turn the pig right side out and press. Stuff through the opening E–F–G. Slipstitch the opening.

13 Satin stitch two nostrils on the smaller fabric circle. Glue the smaller cardboard circle to the wrong side of it. Snip the fabric. Slipstitch the snout into the opening for it, tucking in the raw edges as you go.

14 Make and attach the four foot pads in the same way.

15 Hand sew the ears to the head in the position shown on the pattern.

MATERIALS

- ½ yard chintz 45 inches wide
- Sewing thread to match
- Thin cardboard
- One pair ⅜ inch safety eyes
- About 20 ounces polyester stuffing
- White glue
- Embroidery floss in black

DYED
IN THE
WOOL

This handsome needlepoint hog is obviously a dyed-in-the-wool gourmand. Contentedly munching his meal, he has everything a fellow could want — a ready supply of food, with acorns easily to hand, plus a nice comfy house and some glorious mud. The rich, somber colors of this lovely needlepoint pillow give the scene a peaceful feeling. Stitched entirely in half cross-stitch, it shows how an intricate design can be achieved with one simple stitch. If you already have experience of needlepoint, it offers an excellent opportunity to show off your skills. And if you have never tried needlepoint before, this project is the perfect introduction.

Finished size approximately 12 inches square

MATERIALS

- 16 inch square of 12-gauge interlock canvas
- Tapestry yarns
- Tapestry needle, size 20
- Masking tape or bias binding (optional)
- Waterproof marker
- Needlepoint frame (optional – see Tips)
- ⅓ yard medium-weight, firmly woven furnishing fabric

WORKING THE STITCHES

1 Mark the center of the canvas with a waterproof marker. There are 149 stitches to each side. It is easiest to count outward from the center; there will be 74 threads on each side of the central one, both widthwise and lengthwise. There are 48 stitches between the center stitch and the inner black border.

2 This project is worked in half cross-stitch over one thread of the canvas. Each square of the chart represents a stitch. (Do not use tent stitch with it, even though they look the same from the front, or the surface will be uneven.)

3 Cut a length of brown yarn no more than about 20 inches long. To thread the needle, loop one end of the yarn around the sharp end of the needle. Now, holding it between your thumbnail and first finger, push the doubled end through the eye of the needle.

4 Knots lead to problems when stretching the work at the end so the ends of the yarn are woven in at the back instead. When starting a new length, tie a "waste" knot in the end, then take the needle down from above the canvas, about 2 inches away from where the first stitch will be, so the "tail" of the yarn will be in the path of your first stitches. Once the tail is covered by these stitches, snip off the knot at the front.

5 To make the first stitch, bring the needle up through the hole at the bottom left of the central point. Take it diagonally over one canvas intersection to upper right. Insert it under one horizontal thread and bring the needle out at the front to begin the next stitch. Continue working half cross-stitch in this way along the row from left to right.

6 At the end of the row, turn the canvas around 180° and work back, again from left to right.

7 You can also work it vertically. Simply take the stitch under a vertical thread from right to left, instead of under a horizontal one.

8 When working each stitch, you can use the "stabbing" method, in which the two movements involved in each stitch are done one at a time (best when using a frame) or the "sewing" method in which the movements are done in one scooping movement. Avoid pulling the yarn too tightly. To allow the yarn to untwist, let the needle dangle frequently.

9 As you finish the length of yarn, fasten off by darning it into the underside of the work. It is easiest to work all the nearby stitches of a particular color at once before changing to a different color. If you wish to use the same color in a different area that is not too far away, thread the yarn through the underside of the adjacent stitches to take it to that area.

- 24 inch square of thick wood (see Tips)
- 24 inch square of undyed cotton fabric
- Hammer and 50–60 rustproof nails or tacks
- Sewing thread in black, to match border
- Two small pieces of cardboard (such as small index cards)
- 12 inch pillow form

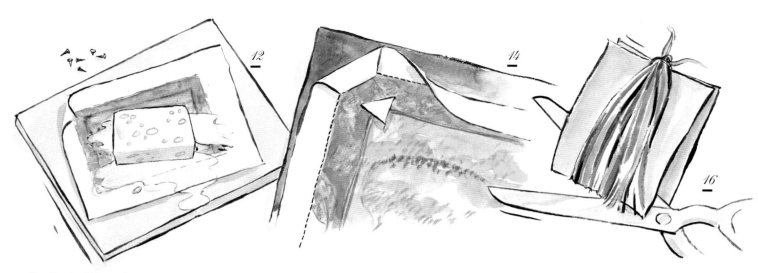

10 Gradually work outward from the center until you get to the borders. After working the picture and the inner borders, work the leaves and acorns, repeating the section shown on the chart, then the gray behind them, and finally the outer borders.

BLOCKING AND SETTING

11 Most needlepoint projects need to be "blocked and set," so the edges are straight, the corners square, the surface smooth, and the pattern not distorted. If your work has not distorted, simply pressing it on the wrong side with a steam iron may be sufficient. Otherwise, you will need to follow step 12.

12 Place the cotton fabric on the piece of wood, then lay the needlepoint face down on top. Dampen the back. Stretching the work so the corners are square, hammer in the nails at ¾ inch intervals. Leave to dry for at least 48 hours, then remove the nails.

MAKING UP THE PILLOW

13 Cut out the backing fabric so that it is the same size as the worked area, plus ⅝ inches all around.

14 Pin the backing to the needlepoint with right sides together. Trim off excess canvas. Stitch close to the needlepoint all around the edges, leaving a gap in the bottom edge. Trim the corners.

TASSELS

15 Cut two pieces of cardboard slightly longer than the desired length of the tassel. Place together and wind lengths of yarn around them.

16 When the yarn is the desired thickness, cut the yarn, laying the ends flat and even with one edge of the cardboard. Slide a new length of yarn through the loops at one end, between the pieces of cardboard. Tie in a knot. Cut the loops at the opposite end, passing the scissors blade between the pieces. Remove the cardboard.

17 Fold the lengths of yarn to the other side, over the knot. Bind about one-fifth of the way down from the top with a 10 inch length of yarn. Thread it through the tapestry needle and take it through the center of the top of the tassel. Now thread this through one corner of the pillow and sew to the canvas inside.

FINISHING

18 Turn the cover right side out, insert the pillow form and hand sew the opening. If you need to remove the cover for cleaning, these stitches can be unpicked and then resewn.

TIPS

• A needlepoint frame is not essential for working this project, but it makes the stitching easier and reduces distortion.

• Before using the waterproof marker, double-check on a scrap of canvas that it definitely is waterproof, otherwise the color might bleed when you dampen the work to block and set it.

• The wood you use for blocking and setting must be unpainted, unstained, and unvarnished.

KEY

Color	DMC no.	Color	DMC no.
mid gray	7620	dark green	7387
light gray	7618	pale green	7703
dark brown	7488	olive green	7364
mid brown	7518	pale pink	7260
black	7309	dark pink	7264
yellow	7485	beige	7415
orange	7444	light beige	7463
browny		mauve	7266
pink	7217	blue	7555
		cream	7300

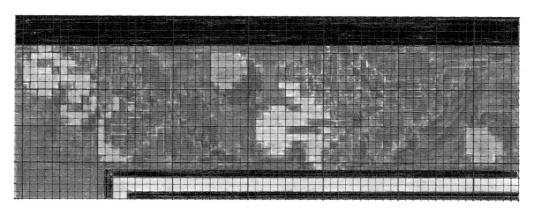

CENTER

CENTER

NUTS ABOUT PIGS

No doubt these hungry hogs are planning to feast on the acorns they see all about them. And it's not just the animals who are dazzled: The generous proportions and bright, contrasting colors of this quilted wallhanging give it enormous impact. Perhaps the most charming aspect is the use of padding for the pigs themselves, creating a rounded, three-dimensional effect which accentuates their porkiness. The project is designed as a large wallhanging, but by changing the proportions and enlarging it, you could turn it into a spectacular quilted bedspread.

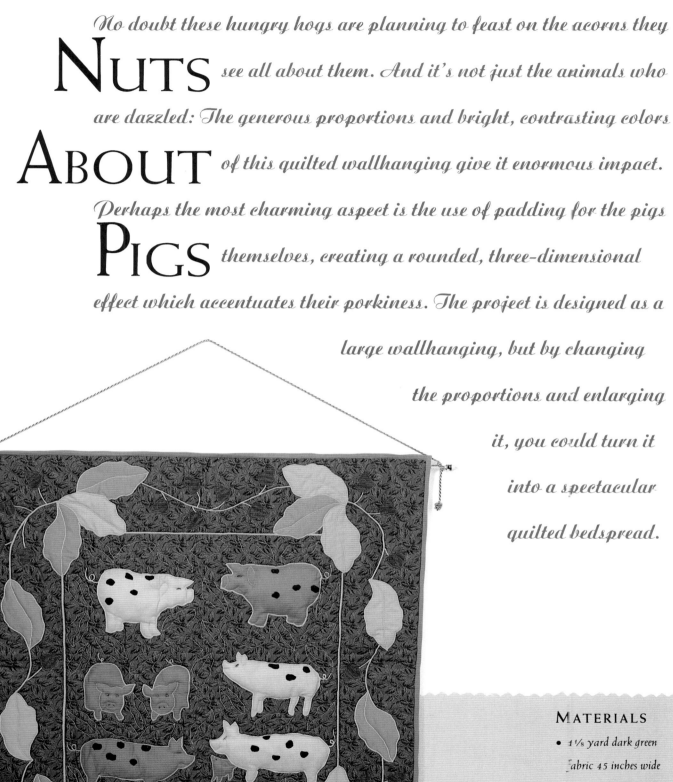

Finished size 34 inches square

MATERIALS

- 1⅛ yard dark green fabric 45 inches wide
- 1⅛ yard firm backing fabric 45 inches wide
- 1⅛ yard lightweight fabric (such as fine

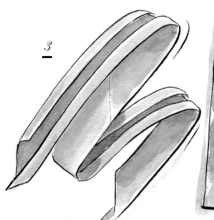

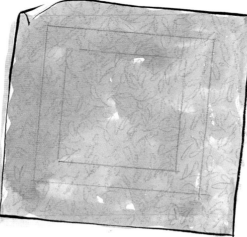

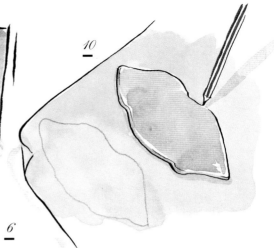

CUTTING OUT AND PREPARATION

1 Using the patterns on pages 116–17, cut out seven adult pigs and one piglet. You will need one each of some patterns and two of others (with the second in reverse). Four of the shapes plus the piglet should be in dark pink, and the other three in light pink.

2 Using the acorn and leaf patterns on the same page, cut out eight leaves (half of them in reverse) from mid green fabric, and the same from light green fabric. Cut out 28 acorns from brown fabric.

3 From the dark pink fabric, make up four 1½ inch wide strips of bias binding (page 106), each 39 inches long. Turn under and press ¼ inch on the long edges.

4 Following the manufacturer's directions, iron fusible web to the wrong side of the black fabric square, then cut out 22 irregularly shaped "spots" about ¾ x ⅜ inch. Remove the backing and iron the spots to the right sides of the pig shapes.

5 Cut a 39 inch square from the dark green fabric. Fold it into quarters to find the center, and mark with a pin.

6 Working from the center outward and using a soft, light pencil, mark an inner square and an outer square on the fabric. The inner square should have 21 inch sides and the outer square 34 inch sides. The 6½ inch wide oak leaf and acorn border will go between the inner and outer squares. The outer square will be the actual edge of the finished quilt, but do not cut off the excess fabric yet.

7 From the firm backing fabric, cut a 39 inch square and a 39 x 5 inch rectangle.

8 From the lightweight fabric, cut a 39 inch square.

ARRANGING THE DESIGN

9 Using the photograph of the finished quilt as a guide, position the pigs, leaves, and acorns on the quilt. When you are happy with their positions (which do not have to be identical to those in the project) pin and baste them.

10 Using the pattern on page 117, make a template of the leaf quilting design from a piece of cardboard. Use this to mark out the quilting design randomly around the pigs.

11 Draw the stem design onto the border, using the photograph of the wallhanging as a guide.

- muslin) 45 inches wide
- 39 inch square of lightweight batting, plus scraps of batting
- ½ yard dark pink fabric 45 inches wide
- 20 x 12 inches light pink fabric
- 16 x 20 inches mid green fabric
- 16 x 20 inches light green fabric
- 12 x 8 inches brown fabric
- 6 inch square of black fabric
- Sewing thread
- 6 inch square of fusible web
- 38 inch dowel
- 1⅛ yard pink cord

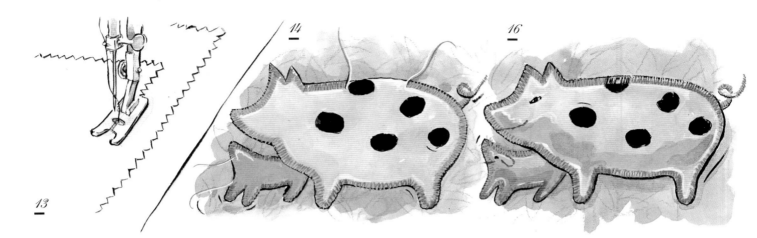

ASSEMBLING THE QUILT

12 Place the lightweight fabric on a flat surface with the batting on top. Lay the top piece over this, right side up. Pin or baste through all three layers, all over the quilt.

13 To minimize fabric distortion and "shrinkage," first stitch around the inner square and then around the outer square, using a narrow zigzag stitch. (This stitching will not actually show.)

EMBROIDERING THE PIGS

14 To appliqué the pigs, set your machine for a medium satin stitch ⅛ inch wide. Stitch around the outline of each pig, leaving a gap at the top (at the throat for the piglet). Use the same width of stitch to embroider the curly tails.

15 With a small crochet hook or the tip of a pencil, push little pieces of batting into each pig, stuffing them lightly. Machine satin stitch the gaps, using the ⅛ inch stitch width as before.

16 Embroider the ears, mouths, and legs of the four pigs that are in profile using pink thread and a narrow satin stitch – fractionally over ¹⁄₁₆ inch. This requires patience, as you are sewing through very fat pigs! Embroider their eyes by hand, using black thread. For the two pigs facing front, use the narrow satin stitch for the heads, hand embroider the eyes and nostrils in black, and use a straight machine stitch and pink thread for the snouts and mouths. For the piglet, hand embroider the black eyes, and use straight machine stitch in pink for the snout, mouth, and ear.

EMBROIDERING THE LEAVES AND ACORNS

17 Using the ⅛ inch wide satin stitch, appliqué the leaves and acorns by stitching all around the edges. (There is no need to leave a gap, as these will not be padded.)

18 Use the same stitch width to embroider the stems all around the border.

19 Reduce the stitch width to ⅛ inch and embroider the vein down the center of each leaf.

COMPLETING THE QUILTING

20 Using a narrow satin stitch – just under ¹⁄₁₅ inch – carefully quilt the random leaf shapes you marked on the background fabric. This will be easier if you use free-style embroidery (page 109).

TIPS

• Fusible web will hold the pigs' spots in place, but, if you prefer, you could attach the spots by sewing a small black circle in the middle of each spot.

• When marking the green fabric, you should not cut off the excess fabric – machine embroidery can "shrink" fabric and you may need to adjust the

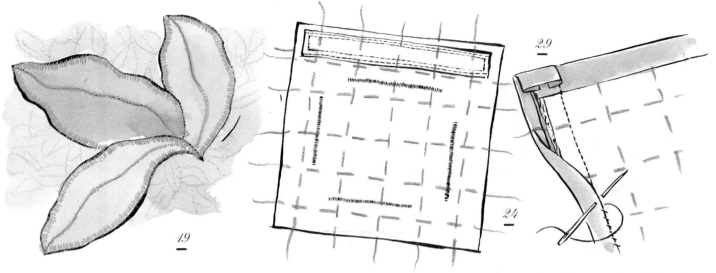

19

29

24

BACKING THE QUILT

21 Trim the backing fabric so that it is the same size as the quilt. Trim the 5 inch wide strip so that it is the same length as the width of the quilt.

22 Turn under all four edges of this strip by ½ inch, press, then turn under the same amount again and press. Machine (straight) stitch along the fold on all four sides.

23 Pin the strip along the top of the backing, 1 inch from the top edge and centered between the other two edges. Stitch along the top and bottom edges of the strip, leaving the sides unstitched. This forms a casing for the dowel.

24 With wrong sides together, pin and baste the backing to the quilt top. Using a wide satin stitch – approximately 3/16 inch wide – stitch over the inner square through all layers.

BINDING THE EDGES

25 With right sides together and raw edges even, pin the bias binding to the top of the quilt, along one edge. Stitch, taking a ¼ inch seam (in other words, stitching along the pressed fold).

26 Trim away excess binding at both ends and also excess batting or backing.

27 Turn the binding to the back. With the other pressed seam allowance turned under, pin and then hemstitch the binding in place.

28 Repeat steps 25–27 for the opposite edge.

29 For the other two sides, follow the procedure in step 25. Trim away excess binding, backing, or batting, leaving about 1 inch excess binding at each end. Turn in the ends, wrapping the extra binding around the corner. Now turn the binding over to the back, and hemstitch it in place as in step 27.

30 Remove the basting. Slot the dowel through the casing at the top of the backing, and tie the cord to each end of the dowel for hanging.

quilt size when all the embroidery is finished.

• A narrow curtain rod with finials instead of a wooden dowel adds an elegant touch.

Piggies in the Middle

No one who loves doing cross-stitch embroidery could resist the beribboned pair of pink porkers featured in this pretty sampler. And, for good measure, the border is made up of their family, a whole cavalcade of fat little piglets standing to attention around all four edges. The sampler is worked almost entirely in cross-stitch – with the main exception being sixteen curly tails which are worked, appropriately enough, in backstitch.

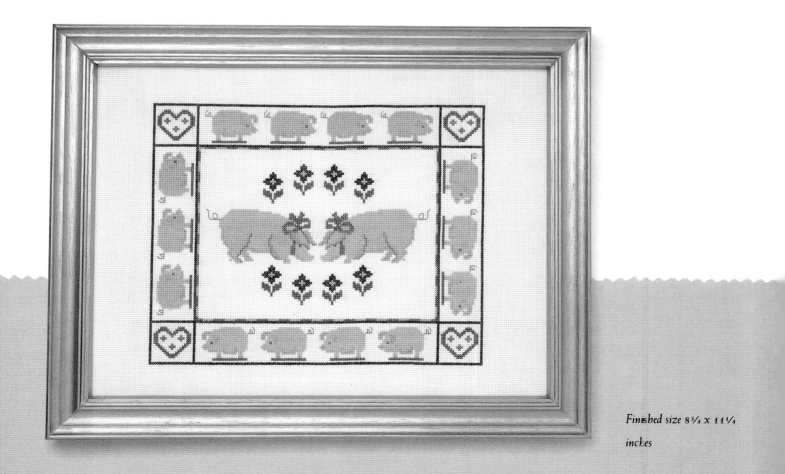

Finished size 8¾ x 11¼ inches

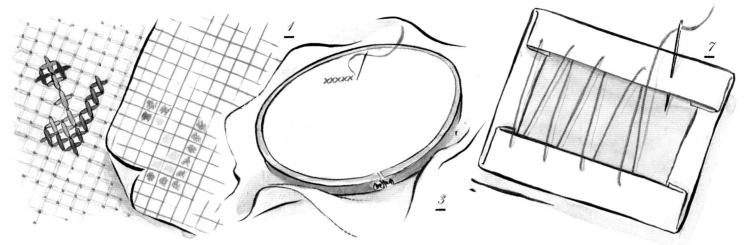

PREPARATION

1 The design is worked over 126 holes high by 153 holes wide. There is a margin of 2 inches of extra fabric all around. If you want to make your sampler larger, simply use a fabric with fewer threads per inch, which means that the stitches will be bigger. Or, if you would like it to be smaller, use one with a higher count, ie more threads per inch and therefore smaller stitches. If, for example, you used 22-count fabric rather than 14-count, the stitch size and the new dimensions would be about two-thirds those of the original.

2 Find and mark the center point by folding the fabric in half lengthwise and running a basting thread along the fold between the threads, and then doing the same crosswise. Where the two threads cross is the center, which corresponds to the center point indicated on the chart (pages 38–9).

EMBROIDERY

3 On the chart, each square represents one cross-stitch, and each symbol indicates the color it should be. All the cross-stitches are worked using two strands of embroidery floss. Be sure to use a hoop when working this sampler. Not only will it prevent distortion, but it is also much easier to work.

4 Following the hand embroidery instructions on page 108 and the Stitch Glossary on page 110, begin stitching the cross-stitch from the center point, changing colors of embroidery floss as necessary.

5 Once the stitching is complete, add the backstitch detail on the central pigs, and all the pigs' tails, worked in one strand of deep rust.

FINISHING

6 On completion, press the embroidery lightly on the wrong side, as directed on page 108.

7 To prepare the sampler for framing, cut a piece of hardboard or strong cardboard to the size of the frame. Place this on the wrong side of the embroidery. Check that it is absolutely square and centered, then secure it in position with pins along the edges. Fold two opposite edges of the fabric over the hardboard. With long lengths of strong thread, lace back and forth, pulling tightly to stretch the fabric. Repeat for the remaining edges.

MATERIALS

- 15 x 12½ inches Aida, 14-count, in cream
- Stranded embroidery floss: 16¼ yards pink, 6½ yards red, 5½ yards orange, 2¼ yards deep rust, 3¼ yards green, and 1 yard blue
- Tapestry needle, size 24
- Embroidery hoop
- Strong cardboard or hardboard, for mounting (optional)
- Strong sewing thread, for mounting (optional)

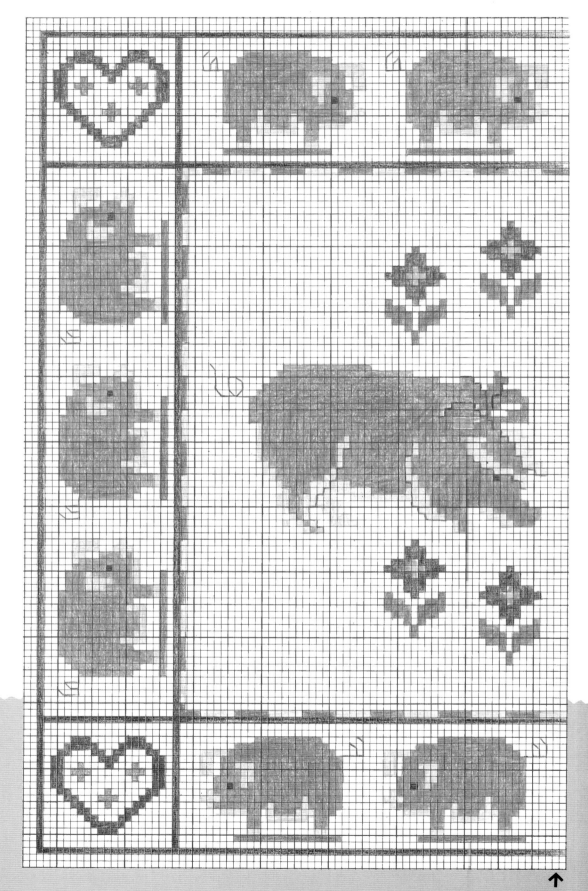

CENTER

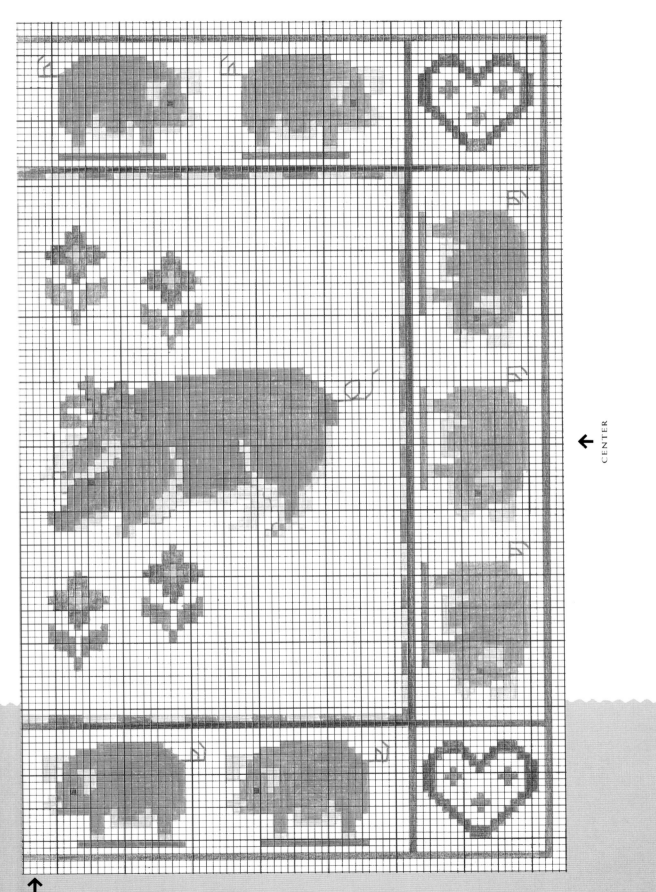

CENTER

PRACTICAL PIGS

The work of teaching and organizing fell naturally upon the pigs, who were generally recognized as being the cleverest of animals.

George Orwell, *Animal Farm*

CHECK MATES

Brighten up the kitchen with this cheerful check pot holder and matching dish towel. A small-scale Shaker check fabric is the starting point — here it has been used for the dish towel and for the trim on the pot holder, with a larger, coordinating check for the pot holder itself. For decoration, you can use either appliquéd pigs in the coordinating fabric (as on the pot holder) or embroidered pigs in cross-stitch (as on the dish towel). Both methods are shown here, but you may prefer to have the same form of decoration for the pair.

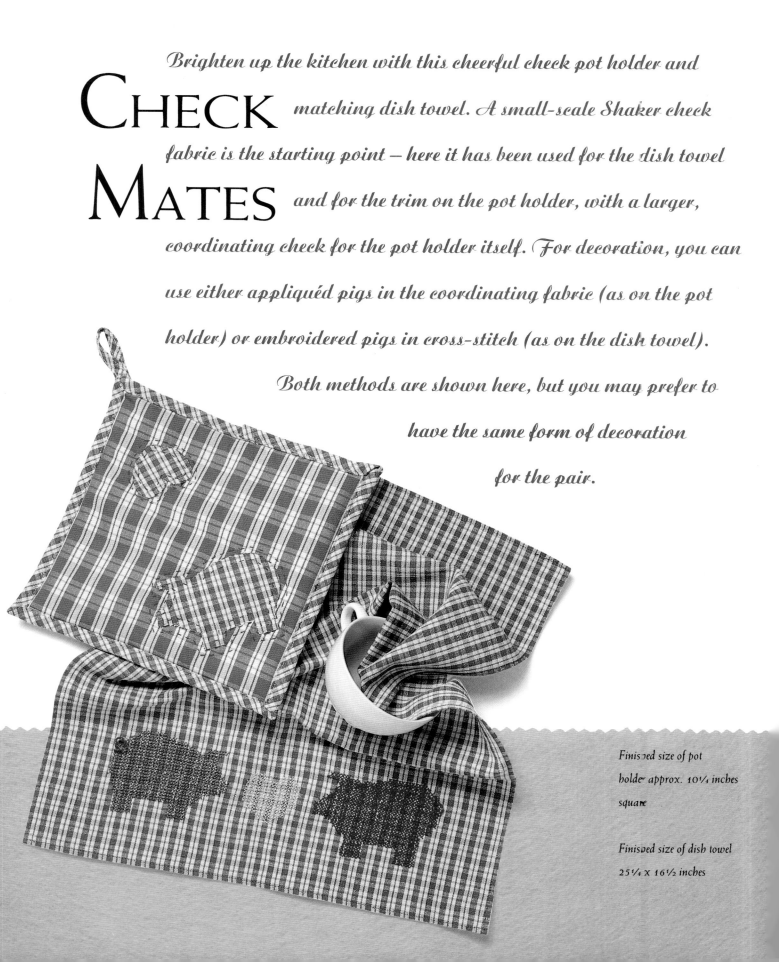

Finished size of pot holder approx. 10¼ inches square

Finished size of dish towel 25¼ x 16½ inches

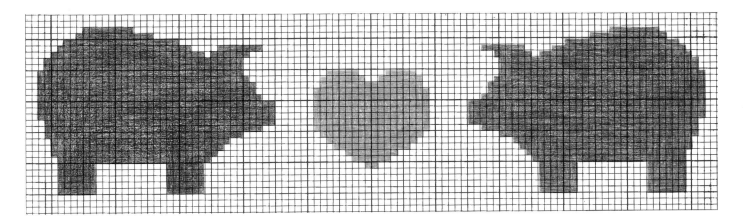

CUTTING OUT THE POT HOLDER

1 Using the patterns on page 121, draw the pig and heart on the paper backing of the fusible web. (The pig will be in reverse.) Cut out the shapes roughly and iron them onto the wrong side of the smaller-check fabric, following the manufacturer's directions. Now cut the shapes out exactly.

2 From the smaller-check fabric, cut out and join 2½ inch wide bias strips until you have a continuous strip about 49 inches in length (page 106).

MAKING THE POT HOLDER

3 Peel the backing from the pig and heart and fuse them to the right side of diagonally opposite corners of one of the larger-scale check squares, about 2 inches in from the edges, and positioned across the corners.

4 Pin the batting to the wrong side of the appliquéd fabric. Using the red embroidery thread, work running stitch around each motif, ¼ inch inside and outside the edge, and also just outside the edge. Alternatively, if you wish to cover the raw edges to prevent possible raveling, machine satin stitch around the motif edges.

5 With wrong sides together, pin this square to the other fabric square. Baste all around the edges.

6 Fold the bias binding strips lengthwise so that the raw edges meet in the center, and press. Now fold the bias strip in half lengthwise and press.

7 Pin the bias binding all around the edge of the pot holder, enclosing the raw edges. Stitch in place, neatly turning under the raw end of the binding.

8 From an 8 inch length of the remaining binding, make up a hanging loop and hand sew this to the back of the pot holder at the corner with the heart.

MAKING THE DISH TOWEL

9 Turn under a double ¼ inch hem all around; pin and stitch.

10 Using the patterns on page 121, transfer one heart and two pig shapes (one in reverse) onto waste canvas.

11 Position the pieces of waste canvas about 2 inches from one short edge of the check fabric, and centered between the long edges. Baste firmly.

12 Placing each motif in the hoop in turn, work the patterns shown in cross-stitch above. Be careful to work through the fabric too.

13 When all the motifs have been stitched, carefully pull out the waste-canvas threads, one thread at a time. Remove all those in one direction, then all those in the opposite direction.

14 For each tail, braid four strands of red embroidery thread with two strands of blue. Thread the braid into the end of each pig, so both ends are fastened down, with a loop between. Fasten off on the wrong side.

MATERIALS

For pot holder

- ¼ yard of smaller-scale check fabric
- Two 11 inch squares of larger-scale check fabric
- Sewing thread to match
- Fusible web
- No. 16 brilliant embroidery thread in red
- 11 inch square of medium batting

For dish towel

- 26 x 17½ inch piece of smaller-scale check fabric
- Waste canvas, 8.5 count
- No. 16 embroidery cotton, in red, blue, and pink
- Sewing thread to match
- Embroidery hoop

HOT STUFF

Keep your coffee hot and your tabletop cool with this quilted French press cover and matching set of coasters. These are made from a novelty pig print fabric, then quilted and piped in pink to match the pigs. The check pattern is perfect for quilting, but you could equally well use a completely different pig- motif fabric. You may even be able to find some Teflon®-coated fabric, which is particularly heat-resistant. The coasters are also ideal for preventing the moisture on cold glasses from marking the tabletop.

Finished size of coasters
4⅛ inches

Finished size of French press cover 14⅜ x 6½ inches – to fit standard eight-cup French press

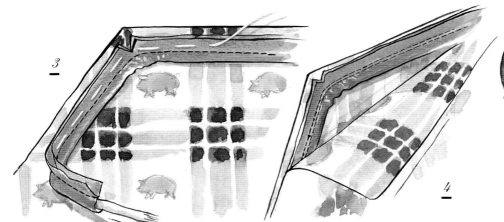

3

4

9

CUTTING OUT

1 Using the pattern on page 115, cut out two French press cover pieces from the fabric and one piece from the batting.

2 For the coasters, use a circle 4¾ inches in diameter as a pattern. Cut out two circles for each coaster.

MAKING THE FRENCH PRESS COVER

3 Cover the piping cord with the bias binding. Pin and then baste the piping all around the edge of one cover piece on the right side, with the raw edges even, clipping into the piping seam allowance on corners. Join the ends of the piping together (page 107). With the zipper foot or piping foot on your sewing machine, stitch the piping in place.

4 Pin the other cover piece to the first, with right sides together. Still using the zipper foot or piping foot, stitch all around the edges, leaving an opening for turning. (Be careful to stitch just outside the stitching line of the piping, so that it will not show on the completed cover.) Trim the seam and turn right side out.

5 Slide the batting inside the cover through the opening, making sure it is completely smooth.

6 Turn in the raw edges of the opening and slipstitch it closed.

7 Quilt the cover by topstitching in the contrasting thread, following the check pattern if you are using a check fabric. If you are using a different fabric, either follow suitable lines of the design, or create your own stitching guide by sticking on lengths of masking tape at regular intervals and removing each one after you have stitched alongside it. Carefully tie the thread ends on the underside.

8 Hand sew the two snaps onto the ends of the French press cover, just inside the piping, sewing the "hole" part of the snap on the right side of the underlap, and the "ball" part of the snap on the wrong side of the overlap.

9 Make up two pink bows and hand-sew them over the snaps on the right side of the overlap.

MAKING THE COASTERS

10 Pipe the edge of the coasters and then make them up in the same way as the French press cover, steps 3–7.

MATERIALS

- ⅝ *yard of 36 inch wide fabric with small pig motif*
- *Sewing thread to match and to contrast*
- *Fine piping cord*
- *Plain 1¼ inch wide bias binding in a contrasting color*
- *Batting*
- *Narrow pink ribbon*
- *Two snaps*

PIGS ON THE TABLE

Stenciling a border with fabric paints is a quick way of adding decoration to a table runner. You could make one to fit a particular side table, coffee table, or chest-of-drawers — or make one long enough for the dining room table by simply increasing the number of repeated images. After all, what better motif is there for the dinner table than lines of fat little pigs? You could also edge a set of placemats in the same way, or stencil a border along the hem of a tablecloth, a shade, or kitchen curtains. The stenciled fabric can be washed in cold water, but to be safe wash it separately, at least at first. Do not soak for long or wring it out.

Finished size 26½ x 12 inches.

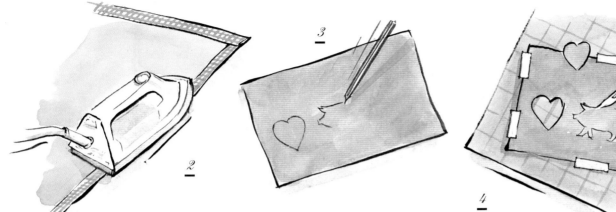

If you wish to alter the size of the runner, or use this stencil on something else, make sure that the motifs will fit into the dimensions exactly. The pattern repeat is 6 inches, and you need to allow an extra 2½ inches so that you can both start and finish with a heart. The finished length of the fabric, therefore, needs to be equal to the number of repeats times 6 inches, plus 2½ inches. For example, this runner has four repeats and an extra heart on the right, so the length is 4 x (6 inches + 2½ inches) = 26½ inches.

MAKING THE RUNNER

1 Wash, dry, and iron the fabric, in order to remove any size or other finishes, as these could cause the paint to spread on the surface.

2 Cut a 28½ x 14 inch rectangle of fabric. Press under a ⅜ inch hem all around, then a further ⅝ inch. Stitch. Press the completed runner.

CUTTING THE STENCIL

3 Transfer the stencil design on page 119 to stencil card or Mylar®. Be sure to leave at least a 1 inch margin all around the design, to strengthen the stencil and also stop paint from being accidentally brushed over the edge of the stencil onto the fabric.

4 Tape the stencil card to a cutting mat, piece of wood, or thick layer of newspapers. Use a sharp, lightweight craft knife (which is easier to manipulate than a heavy one) to carefully cut out the design. To cut the stencil, hold the craft knife in one hand and place your free hand on the stencil, with your fingers pointing away from where you will be cutting. Holding the knife almost straight up and down, cut toward you along the line, almost as though you were drawing with the knife. Try to keep the edges as smooth as possible, to give a sharper image. Any repairs to the stencil can be done with a small piece of masking tape stuck on either side of the card.

5 Mark a line about ⅜ inch from the edge of the design, which is where the edge of the fabric will be positioned.

MATERIALS

- ½ yard fabric 36 inches wide
- Sewing thread to match
- 13¼ x 3½ inch piece of oiled manila stencil card or Mylar®
- Craft knife
- Low-tack spray adhesive
- Masking tape
- Stencil brush
- Fabric paints in two

shades of pink, two shades of red, and brown (see Tips)

POSITIONING THE STENCIL

6 The stencil needs to be fixed securely to the fabric so that it is both immovable and as flat as possible, otherwise you could get a blurry image. The best way to do this is to use a low-tack spray adhesive. Working in a well-ventilated room, spray the back of the stencil with the spray adhesive. You don't need to use much, but it is important to get an even coverage over the whole stencil. The adhesive needs to be strong enough to hold the stencil on the fabric but weak enough to allow it to be peeled off easily.

7 Use masking tape to anchor the fabric to several sheets of newspaper or some thick cardboard on the work surface. Place the stencil firmly down on the fabric, with the design the right way around (in other words, not reversed). Position the stencil at the left-hand side so that the point of the first heart is 1¼ inches from the left-hand edge.

STENCILING THE DESIGN

8 Pour a little of each of the paint colors around a saucer or plate. Stencil a test piece of fabric before stenciling the runner itself, to check the colors and practice the technique. When in use, the stencil brush must never be damp or wet, or the design will be blurred. Charge the brush with paint, then rub off the excess onto the plate or saucer, so that the brush is quite dry. Using too much paint will cause it to seep underneath the stencil and smudge the design. It's better to build up the color gradually.

9 Holding the brush like a pen, make short, up-and-down jabbing movements onto the fabric from directly above, so that the bristles do not go under the stencil (which would create a fuzzy, messy outline). This technique is known as pouncing.

TIPS

• It's important to use a non-stretchy fabric, since stretching can cause the stencil design to smudge. A closely woven cotton is best.

• The paints need to be fairly thick, rather than a runny consistency, so that they will not seep under the stencil and cause smudging.

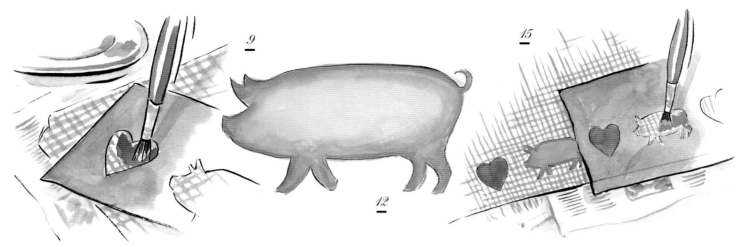

10 Once you feel you have the knack, begin stenciling the actual runner. For the first pig, apply the lighter pink as a base coat. If the fabric is a strong color, you may need to apply a second coat after the first one has dried (in which case do not lift the stencil between coats).

11 Using the second brush, apply the lighter red as a base coat for the first two hearts. Allow to dry for a couple of minutes.

12 Using the first brush again and without removing the stencil, apply a deeper pink and a little brown as shading on the pig, concentrating it around the edges of the animal to give a more three-dimensional effect. This makes the pig look more rounded and interesting.

13 Using the second brush again, apply the deeper red paint all over the hearts.

14 Carefully peel the stencil off the fabric, lifting it straight up rather than sliding it, which could smudge the design. Wipe the stencil clean if necessary.

15 Now place the stencil in the next position, with the left-hand heart over the one you have just stenciled. (Though overlapping the stencil in this way is not quite as quick as moving the whole stencil along to the next position, it ensures accurate placement.) Continue in the same way until both edges of the runner have been stenciled.

FINISHING

16 When you have finished stenciling and the paint is dry, fix the paints according to the manufacturer's directions (probably by ironing with a hot iron on both sides of the fabric for several minutes).

17 If you wish to save the stencil for re-use, clean it first and then put talcum powder on the back and store it between sheets of stencil card, keeping it flat.

SHOWING THE DOOR

So appealing is this podgy pig doorstop that it is perfectly capable of stopping not only doors but people, who can't resist giving this adorable hog a hug as they pass by. With its plaid covering and velvety ears and snout, it looks very smart but would also look good in a fabric to match the decor of the room. Care is required when cutting out plaid fabric to insure that it matches all around and is symmetrical, so you may prefer to use a fabric that does not require matching. However, the dramatic effect of the plaid is worth the effort!

Finished size approximately 10½ inches tall x 7 inches deep x 6 inches wide excluding "arms" or 14 inches including "arms"

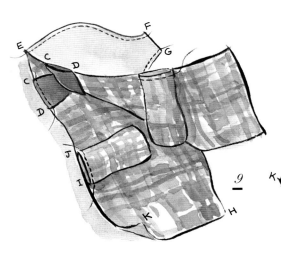

9

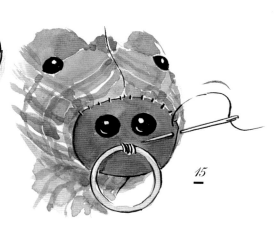

11

15

1 Using the patterns on page 126, cut out from main fabric two body fronts (one in reverse), two body backs (one in reverse) and four "arms."

2 Also from the main fabric, cut a 7 inch circle for the base and two 4 inch squares for the weights.

3 From velvet cut out four ears (two in reverse) and two snout pieces.

4 From fusible interfacing cut out all the pieces you cut in step 1. Fuse to the wrong side of each piece.

MAKING THE EARS, ARMS, AND EYES

5 With right sides together, stitch two ear pieces from point D down one side and up the other to point C, taking an ⅛ inch seam. Clip the curves. Turn right side out but do not press. Repeat for the other ear.

6 Join arm pieces between I and J as for the ears. Stuff, then stitch ends.

7 Insert the small eyes on the body where marked (see page 27, step 4).

MAKING THE BODY AND SNOUT

8 With right sides together, stitch ears and arms to right side of body front pieces where shown on pattern.

9 With right sides together, join body front pieces from E–F, and G–H, taking a ¼ inch seam. Clip curves. Press.

10 With right sides together, join body back pieces between A and B, taking a ¼ inch seam. Clip curve. Press.

11 With right sides together, pin back to front at each side, matching A (back) to E (front), and K (back) to K (front). Making sure the ears and arms are inside, stitch each side between A/E and K/K, taking ¼ inch seams. Clip curves, turn right side out, and press.

12 With right sides together, join the snout pieces all around, taking an ⅛ inch seam, and leaving an opening. Turn right side out but do not press. Slipstitch the opening.

13 Insert the larger safety eyes as nostrils in the snout in the same way as the eyes (see page 27, step 4).

14 Hand sew the curtain ring in position beneath the nostrils.

15 Slipstitch the snout into the opening in the seam joining the two front pieces.

STUFFING THE HEAD AND BODY

16 Stuff the head and body with the polyester stuffing through the base. At the base insert a bag made from the two 4 inch fabric squares stitched together and filled with a handful of pebbles.

FINISHING

17 Slipstitch the fabric circle to the base around the bottom edge, turning under the raw edge of the circle as you go.

18 Pull the arms forward a little and secure to the body front with a few hand stitches.

MATERIALS

- ½ yard plaid fabric 36 inches wide, or 45 inches if wide repeat
- 16 x 5 inch piece of velvet
- ½ yard fusible interfacing
- Sewing thread to match
- One pair ⅜ inch black safety eyes
- One pair ½ inch black safety eyes
- 1 inch brass curtain ring
- About 10 ounces polyester stuffing
- Handful of pebbles

PIGS MIGHT FLY

In this wonderful placemat, zingy colors and a whimsical fabric printed with flying pigs are enhanced by the lively pattern of crazy patchwork. The placemat is quilted along the crazy patchwork lines and then the edges are bound.

Traditionally, random-sized and shaped pieces were sewn onto a foundation fabric so that they overlapped each other. However, it is easier to sew the pieces into "block units," with each block built up around a pig motif. The blocks are then sewn together.

Finished size 16½ x 12 inches

MATERIALS

• ¾ yard of novelty cotton fabric with pig motifs, 45 inches wide (more fabric may be necessary if the motifs are widely spaced)

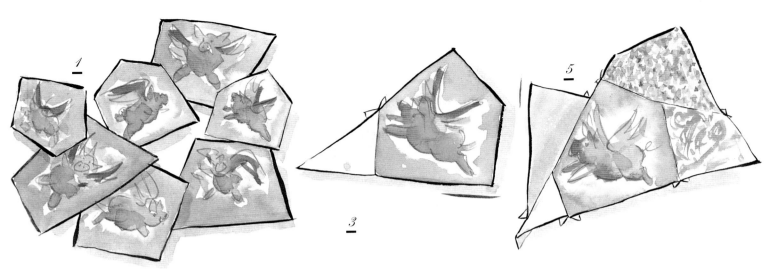

CUTTING OUT THE PATCHES

1 From the pig print fabric, cut out irregular-shaped patches with a pig motif in the center of each. Remember to include a ¼ inch seam allowance all around. Seven pigs were used for this placemat, but the number may vary according to the size of the motif.

2 From the fabric scraps, cut strips measuring approximately 12 x 3 inches.

PIECING THE CRAZY PATCHWORK

3 With this technique, a "pig patch" is the center of a block unit, in which irregular-shaped strips are built up around the pig patch rather like log cabin patchwork. The blocks are then sewn together. With right sides together and raw edges even, pin a strip of scrap fabric to a pig patch along the shortest side of the pig patch. Stitch, taking a ¼ inch seam.

You can either machine stitch these seams, using a medium-length stitch – about 12 stitches to the inch – or sew them by hand. In the latter case, use a small running stitch – about 8–10 stitches to the inch, starting and finishing with a few backstitches. Press the seam and then press the scrap-fabric strip back to its right side. Trim the strip to the required shape and size to create straight lines aligned with the pig patch.

4 With right sides together, pin a second scrap-fabric strip to the pig patch and to the first scrap-fabric patch along an adjacent edge. Stitch, press the seam, turn the new scrap-fabric patch back to its right side, and trim it as before in the same way as you did for the first strip.

5 Continue with the other scrap fabrics, stitching and trimming them into irregular, "crazy" shapes as you build up a block around the central pig motif. Repeat for the other pig motifs.

6 Arrange the blocks into two groups, each of which roughly forms a right-angled triangle.

- Scraps of assorted fabrics, for patches
- ½ yard of plain cotton fabric 45 inches wide, for backing
- ¼ yard of cotton print fabric 45 inches wide, for binding
- Sewing thread to match
- ½ yard of lightweight batting

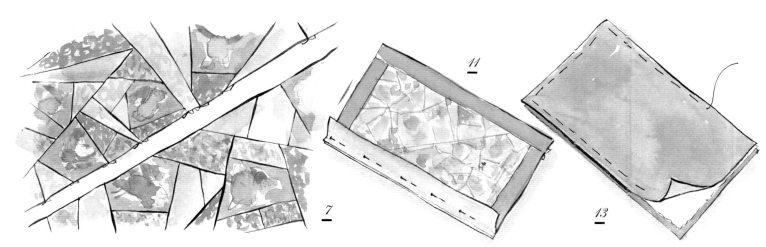

7 Pin and stitch the blocks together, adding extra pieces of fabric where necessary and trimming if required, to complete each triangle. Each of these triangles forms one half of the placemat (divided along the diagonal).

8 With right sides together and raw edges even, pin the two triangles together along the diagonal. Stitch, taking a ⅜ inch seam. Press the seam carefully, taking care not to stretch the fabric on the bias. Trim the fabric if necessary to form a rectangle.

MAKING THE PLACEMAT

9 From the backing fabric, cut two strips the width of the completed crazy patchwork, and two strips the length of the completed patchwork plus 1½ inches.

10 With right sides together and raw edges even, stitch a shorter border strip to each short side of the mat. Press the seam.

11 Stitch the two longer border strips to the longer edges in the same way, so that the ends are flush with the outer edge of the other borders.

QUILTING

12 Cut a piece of batting and a piece of backing fabric to the size of the mat.

13 Sandwich the batting between the patchwork top and the backing fabric. Baste through all layers, so that they will remain smooth rather than developing wrinkles as you quilt.

14 Begin quilting by either hand or machine, stitching around the first pig patch and the "crazy" shapes that connect it to the next motif. It is possible to stitch continuously around each motif and the connecting shapes. To quilt by hand, use a single length of thread and work even running stitches through all three layers. To quilt by machine, reduce the stitch tension if necessary (to prevent puckers), and stitch with a medium straight stitch.

BINDING

15 From the binding fabric, cut two 2½ inch wide strips as long as the width of the placemat, and two strips of the same width that are the length of the placemat plus ½ inch. These can be cut on the straight grain because there are no curves to be bound.

16 Fold each strip in half, wrong sides together, and press.

TIPS

• You don't have to build up a "crazy" log cabin that is too rigid. As you can see, this placemat sometimes has only one piece, rather than two, between the pig motifs. Also, in some places two pieces are used together on one edge of a pig patch. The freer this sort of patchwork is, the better.

• You may find it easier when quilting by hand to start an arm's length away and sew the lines working toward yourself, rather than away.

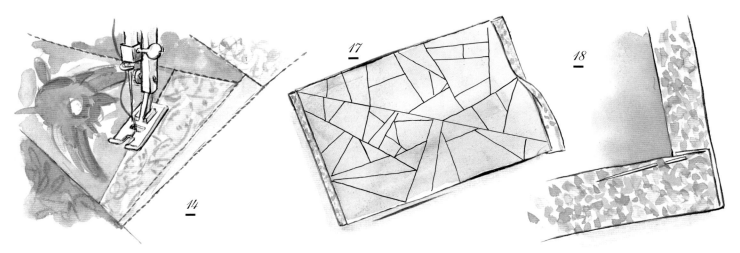

17 With right sides together and raw edges even, stitch a strip of binding (still folded, so that you are stitching through two layers of binding) to each short side of the mat. Press the seam and turn over to the wrong side of the placemat. Slipstitch the folded edge of the binding to the backing fabric, thus creating a double-thickness binding.

18 Repeat the procedure in step 17 with the longer strips of binding, turning under the raw edge of the binding on each corner and hemming to form a neat, finished edge that is flush with the other edges.

VARIATION: CURVED PATCHES
With the method used for this project, the seams have to be straight. If you want to incorporate patches with one or more curved edges, you will need to use the traditional crazy-patchwork method, which is more time-consuming. This technique involves sewing the patches onto a foundation fabric. The patches are not sewn right sides together but are simply laid down, right side up, with the edges overlapping. They have to be cut to approximately the finished shape beforehand.

Cut a patch the full depth of the placemat, shaped like a boot, with a straight top, side, and "sole." Place this with the three straight edges against the edges of the foundation fabric. Baste along all edges.

Position the next piece (which should have at least one straight edge) so that it overlaps the first piece on the latter's curved edge, and so the straight edge is along the straight edge of the

foundation fabric. Turn under the seam allowance on the overlapping edge of the new piece, as this edge will be exposed in the finished placemat.

Continue in this way until the whole foundation piece is covered. Trim the edges to form a rectangle. Slipstitch all the folded edges. Finally, remove the basting and proceed as before.

VARIATION: EMBROIDERED CRAZY PATCHWORK
In its heyday in Victorian times, crazy patchwork was embellished with embroidery. The design of the project placemat is so lively and modern-looking that embroidery could be too much, but a different design may possibly benefit from it. Embroidered crazy patchwork should not be quilted.

One embroidery stitch that was traditionally used for this was feather stitch (see page 110), which is worked along the seamline.

PICTURE OF CONTENTMENT

Three spotted pigs lazing peacefully in the straw decorate this pretty picture frame. Both the frame and the appliquéd pigs are made from silk, and, incongruous though it may seem, the effect is surprisingly delicate and elegant. Indeed, the traditional association of sows' ears with silk is rather more successful here than in the old adage about silk purses. If, however, you prefer a less luxurious look, you could use a different fabric — for example, a plaid cotton or check gingham with felt pigs.

Finished size 10 x 8 inches; window size 5¾ x 4 inches

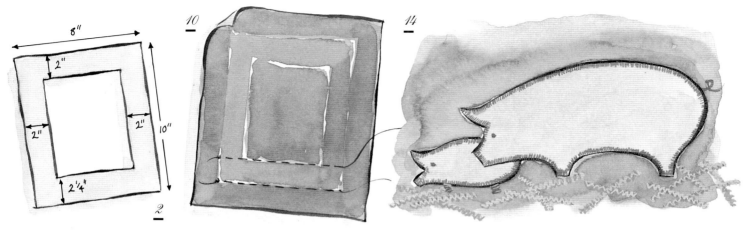

CUTTING OUT AND PREPARATION

1 Using a sharp craft knife, cut a 10 x 8 inch piece of hardboard for the back of the frame and a 6 x 2 inch piece for the strut.

2 Still using the craft knife, cut a 10 x 8 inch piece of mounting cardboard for the front of the frame. Carefully measure and mark a 5¾ x 4 inch "window" in this so that the distance from the edge of the frame to the "window" is 2 inches at the top and sides and 2¼ inches at the bottom.

3 Cut two pieces of fabric for the back of the frame: one 14 x 12 inches and one 9 x 7 inches.

4 Cut two pieces of fabric for the strut: one 8 x 4 inches and one 5½ x 1½ inches. Also, cut two 5 x 2¾ inch pieces of fabric for the hinge.

5 Cut one 14 x 12 inch piece of fabric for the front of the frame.

6 Cut a 14 x 12 inch piece of fusible interfacing and, following the manufacturer's directions, iron this onto the wrong side of the fabric for the front. This will prevent the fabric from stretching when you are appliquéing the pigs.

7 Cut a 10 x 8 inch piece of batting for padding the front.

8 Using the patterns on page 119, cut out two adult pigs (one in reverse) and one piglet from the scraps of pink fabric.

9 Following the manufacturer's directions, iron fusible web to the wrong side of a scrap of black fabric. Cut out about seven irregularly shaped spots ranging from approximately ¼ x ⅙ inch to ⅝ x ⅜ inch.

APPLIQUÉ AND EMBROIDERY

10 Using basting stitches, mark out the boundaries for the appliquéd motifs near the bottom of the background fabric for the frame front. Note that there is a 2 inch seam allowance all around the outside edge, and that the bottom part of the frame is 2¼ inches deep.

11 Using a ¹⁄₂₄ inch wide machine satin stitch (page 109) and yellow thread, embroider the straw along the base of the design area.

12 Position the three pigs, and anchor with a few tiny slipstitches around the edge of each.

13 Using a ¹⁄₁₂ inch wide satin stitch and pink thread, stitch around the edges of all three pigs.

14 Hand embroider the eyes and tails of the adult pigs and the eye and legs of the piglet.

MATERIALS

- *Hardboard*
- *Mounting cardboard*
- *⅓ yard rust-colored silk, for background*
- *Scraps of pink silk and black silk, for appliqué*
- *Sewing threads to match pink fabric and in yellow*
- *Medium-weight fusible interfacing*
- *Fusible web*
- *4 ounces batting*
- *White glue*
- *Acetate film*
- *Cellophane tape*

15 Remove the backing from the fusible web on the black spots and fuse them to the pigs.

COVERING THE FRONT OF THE FRAME

16 Glue the batting to the mounting cardboard and trim the batting to the same size. Allow to dry.

17 Remove the basting stitches from the design area. Center the appliquéd fabric over the padded card, making sure that the bottom of the design runs straight along the base of the frame.

18 Cut diagonally across the outer corners within the seam allowances, then fold the excess fabric to the back of the cardboard. Secure at the back with cellophane tape.

19 Working from the back, cut through the fabric of the window in a cross shape, carefully cutting almost, but not quite, into the corners. Trim off the excess fabric on each edge (ie the triangle near the center on each side). Secure the edges at the back with cellophane tape, paying particular attention to the corners.

20 Lift and adjust the fabric around the edge, stretching it slightly to smooth out any wrinkles. Glue into its final position.

21 At the back, stick down all the edges around the window with more cellophane tape, so that these will not be caught when you slide the picture in.

COVERING BACK OF FRAME

22 Lay the larger piece of hardboard centrally on the wrong side of the larger piece of fabric that you cut for the back. Trim the corners of the fabric diagonally within the seam allowance. Stretching the fabric taut, glue the edges to the hardboard. Anchor the fabric with cellophane tape while the glue dries.

23 When the glue is dry, remove the tape. Center the 9 x 7 inch piece of fabric over the hardboard to cover the edges of the previous piece. Hold in place with cellophane tape along each edge of this fabric piece, positioning the tape as far as possible from the edges of the frame back.

TIP

• The hand embroidery used for the tails, eyes, and piglet's legs needs to be very fine. The group of stitches known as backstitches are easy to work and ideal for outlining. Use basic backstitch for straight lines such as the legs, and stem stitch or split stitch for curved lines such as the tails. For the eyes use French knots. All are shown on pages 110–11.

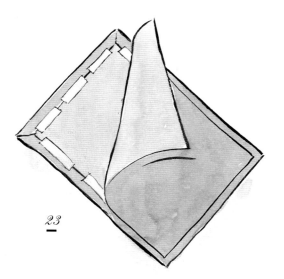

23

26

28

MAKING THE STRUT

24 For the strut, cover the smaller piece of hardboard with the 8 x 4 inch piece of fabric as in step 22. Cover the edges of this piece of fabric with the 5½ x 1½ inch piece of fabric, as in step 23.

ASSEMBLING THE FRAME

25 Glue the frame front to the frame back around the side and bottom edges, leaving the top edge free so that the picture can be inserted later.

26 To make the hinge, fuse the two remaining pieces of fabric together with fusible web. Overlap the short ends by ⅜ inch and hand sew them together. Apply glue to the outside of this fabric ring, leaving 1 inch free of glue. Arrange the ring in a triangular shape with the unglued portion at the base, and glue the other two sides of the triangle to the top of the strut and the center back of the frame.

27 Cut a piece of acetate film slightly larger than the window and slide it through the top edge between the front and back of the frame.

28 Slip a picture down behind the acetate film, trimming it to fit if necessary.

PEARLS BEFORE SWINE

You may prefer not to cast your pearls before swine, but there is no reason why you shouldn't let swine look after them — in the form of a pretty silk trinket box decorated with amiable-looking arimals under a cloudy sky. The box is made using an adaptation of the quilting technique known as trapunto, in which stitched shapes are padded through a slit in the back. The sheen of the silk fabric accentuates the effect, but you could, if you prefer, use a totally different combination of fabrics. The fabric has to be embroidered, appliquéd, and stuffed before being attached to flat pieces of cardboard. These are then shaped into a round, lined box with a neatly fitting lid.

Finished size approximately 3¼ inches in diameter and 2½ inches high.

CUTTING OUT AND PREPARATION

1 Cut a 10¾ x 2¼in inch strip of thin cardboard for the sides of the box and a 11¼ x 1 inch strip for the rim of the lid.

2 Use the two circle patterns on page 119 and a sharp craft knife to cut two circles from mounting cardboard. The smaller one will be the base of the box and the larger one will be the top of the lid.

3 Cut a 12½ x 4¼ inch strip of blue silk to cover the sides of the box and a 13 x 1¾ inch strip to cover the rim of the lid. Cut two 4½ inch circles of blue silk to cover the lid top and box base.

4 For lining the base of the box and the top of the lid, cut two circles from silk to the same size as the cardboard circles. For lining the sides of the box, cut a piece of silk the same size as the wider cardboard strip. Now trim off ¹/₂₄ inch all around each shape.

5 Cut a circle of batting the same size as the larger cardboard circle, for padding the lid.

6 Cut a circle of fusible interfacing the same size as one of the large silk circles, and a strip of fusible interfacing the same size as the larger silk strip. Following the manufacturer's directions, iron the fusible interfacing to the wrong side of these pieces, to prevent them from stretching while the appliqué is being worked.

7 Using the pattern on page 119, cut three pig shapes, all facing in the same direction, from the brown silk.

8 From the white silk, cut out three irregularly shaped clouds, ranging from about 1¼ x ¾ inch to about 1¾ x 1 inch.

9 Following the manufacturer's directions, iron fusible web to a scrap of black silk. Cut out six irregularly shaped spots, ranging from about ⁵/₁₆ inch across to about ⅝ x ⅜ inch.

EMBROIDERY AND APPLIQUÉ

10 With basting stitches, mark the limits of the design on the interfaced fabric strip, allowing 10¼ inches between the two lines. Remember that there will be 1 inch seam allowances at the top and bottom.

11 Use a ¹/₂₄ inch wide machine satin stitch and pink thread to embroider the straw along the bottom of the design area on the silk strip.

MATERIALS

- *Thin, flexible cardboard, for box sides and lid rim*
- *Stiff mounting cardboard, for box base and lid top*
- *¼ yard blue silk*
- *Scraps of brown, black, and white silk*
- *Sewing thread to match brown, white, and blue fabrics and in pink*
- *Medium-weight batting*
- *Medium-weight fusible interfacing*
- *Fusible web*
- *White glue*
- *Cellophane tape*

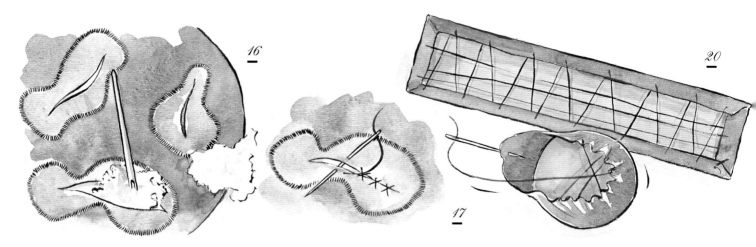

12 Arrange the pig shapes on the embroidered fabric at regular intervals within the design area. Hand sew each in a few places along the edge to anchor them in place. Now machine satin stitch all around the edges, using a $1/12$ inch wide stitch and brown thread. Remove the basting.

13 Remove the fusible web backing from the black spots and fuse two spots to each pig.

14 Appliqué the cloud shapes to the interfaced blue silk circle for the lid in the same way as for the pigs, step 12.

TRAPUNTO

15 Using a small pair of sharp pointed scissors, make a slit in the interfaced fabric behind each pig and cloud shape, being very careful not to cut into the pigs or clouds themselves.

16 Using a darning needle or small crochet hook, push small pieces of batting through each slit to pad the pigs and clouds, gently pushing the batting right into the corners.

HAND SEWING

17 Holding the edges of each slit together, hand sew the slit closed using large cross-stitches. (Do not pull the edges of the opening together or allow them to overlap, or the surface will not be smooth.)

18 Hand embroider the pigs' eyes and tails using tiny French knots and stem stitch or split stitch (see pages 110–11).

COVERING THE BOX

19 For the sides of the box, lay the fabric appliquéd with the pigs wrong side up on the work surface. Place the wider strip of cardboard on it centrally. Trim the corners of the fabric diagonally within the seam allowance, then bring the excess fabric to the back of the cardboard. Pulling the fabric quite taut, lace opposite sides together at the back using a needle and thread.

20 For the base of the box, lay the smaller (unappliquéd) circle of fabric wrong side up on the work surface. Place the smaller cardboard circle centrally on it and bring the excess fabric to the back. Lace together using a needle and thread as in step 19.

TIPS

● Stuffing a shape through a slit in the backing fabric is the traditional way of working trapunto. This is because normally the shape would be built up inside the stitching on two layers of fabric, and access from the front would not be possible. With appliqué, however, you can, if you prefer, simply leave a portion of the satin-stitched outline unstitched at the front, insert the batting through this gap and then complete the stitching.

● Use only tiny pieces of batting to stuff the pigs and clouds, in order to avoid a lumpy effect.

● Do not overstuff the shapes or you could distort the appliqué.

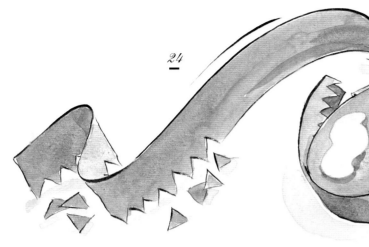

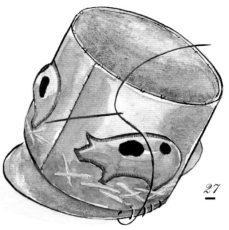

21 Glue the lining pieces to the wrong side of the strip for the box sides and to the wrong side of the circle for the base, covering the lacing. Set aside while you make the lid. (The box cannot be completed until the exact size of the lid is known.)

COVERING THE LID

22 Glue the circle of batting to the cardboard circle for the lid top. When dry, cover with the cloud-appliquéd fabric, as in step 20.

23 Score a line lengthwise along the center of the cardboard strip for the rim of the lid. Fold along the scored line. Open out again. Glue the cardboard centrally to the strip of silk you cut for the rim, wrapping the edges of fabric over to the back of the cardboard. Secure with cellophane tape at the back while the glue dries.

24 When dry, cut the edge of the covered strip in a zigzag pattern, cutting almost up to (but not beyond) the center fold of the cardboard.

25 Fold the cut edge of the covered strip around the edge of the lid top on the underside. Slipstitch it neatly and invisibly.

26 Glue the circular lining piece inside the top of the lid to cover the lacing and the cut edge of the rim.

ASSEMBLING THE BOX

27 Form the appliquéd box side into a cylinder shape that will fit inside the lid exactly. Hand sew at the top of the overlap. Fit the bottom of the cylinder around the base of the box. Slipstitch neatly along the vertical seam on the side of the box and then around where it joins the base.

PERSONAL
PIGS

The sunny slow lulling afternoon yawns and moons through the dozy town . . . Pigs grunt in a wet wallow-bath, and smile as they snort and dream. They dream of the acorned swill of the world, the rooting for pig-fruit . . .

Dylan Thomas, *Under Milk Wood*

HOGWASH

This fun washbag is made from fabric printed with a multitude of smiling pigs, but the theme would come across just as strongly in a plain fabric. Of course, the animal's rounded shape is ideal for such a bag, but even its tail (the rope carrying handle) and nose ring (for pulling the zipper that runs along its spine) are put to good use. Piping in the same fabric runs along the outside and this could, if desired, be made in a contrasting fabric to emphasize the shape.

Finished size 14 x 9 inches

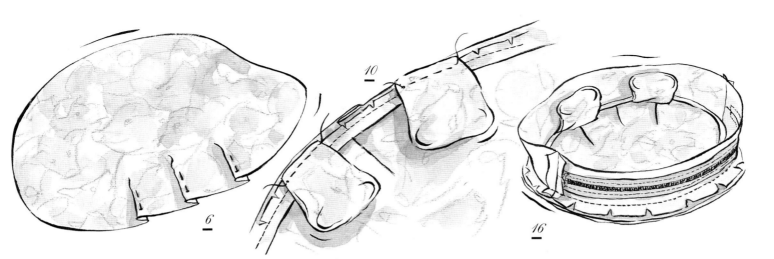

CUTTING OUT

1 Using the patterns on page 127, cut out two bodies and four ears from the main fabric. From the same fabric, cut a 23¾ x 3⅛ inch piece for the base gusset, and two pieces each 14 x 2⅛ inches for the zipper gusset.

2 From the same fabric, cut four 6 x 3½ inch pieces for the legs.

3 From the lining, cut out two body pieces, one base gusset, and two zipper gusset pieces.

4 From the iron-on batting, cut out the same pieces as the main fabric.

MAKING THE BODY

5 Following the manufacturer's directions, fuse the batting to the wrong side of each main fabric piece.

6 Make the three small pleats on each body piece. Pin to hold.

7 Cut strips of bias binding from the fabric and join to make a continuous 2⅛ yard length (page 106).

8 Cover the piping cord with it, then stitch the binding around each body piece (page 107), taking a ⅝ inch seam.

MAKING THE LEGS, EARS, AND EYES

9 Fold each leg piece in half crosswise, with right sides together. Turn up the fold edge for a further ½ inch. Pin and stitch the side edges, taking ⅝ inch seams.

10 Turn right side out, tucking the end up inside the leg to look like a hoof. Position two leg pieces on each body piece, over the piping. Baste in place.

11 With right sides together, join two ear pieces, taking a ⅝ inch seam, and leaving the straight edge open. Trim the seam allowance and turn right side out. Finish edges.

12 Pin and stitch the straight edge of each ear to each body piece. Flop the ears over, and catch down.

13 Sew on buttons for the eyes.

MAKING THE GUSSETS AND LINING

14 Pin and stitch the zipper in between the two zipper gusset pieces (see page 107). Stitch across the ends.

15 Pin, then stitch the base gusset to the zipper gusset at both ends, forming a ring. For the tail fixing, insert an eyelet centrally in the base gusset ¾ inch down from the seam joining it to the zipper gusset.

16 With right sides together and raw edges even, pin and stitch gusset to one body piece, taking a ⅝ inch seam. Open the zipper. Stitch the other side of the gusset to the second body piece in the same way.

17 Make up the plastic lining from the body and gusset pieces as in steps 6, 15, and 16, omitting the zipper.

18 Fit the lining inside the bag with wrong sides together. Turn under the raw edges and slipstitch.

19 Thread the cord through the eyelet. Knot it inside. Put the curtain ring on the zipper end.

MATERIALS

- ⅔ yard cotton fabric 36 inches wide
- 27½ x 23¼ inch piece of thin plastic fabric, for lining
- Sewing thread to match
- Iron-on batting
- 2⅛ yards piping cord
- 2 small buttons, for eyes
- 14 inch zipper
- 1 large eyelet, plus fixing tool
- 13 inch thick white cord (in a thickness that will fit through eyelet)
- 1 curtain ring

CREATURE COMFORTS

Padded coathangers are always an indulgence, particularly when they impart a subtle scent of potpourri to your wardrobe. You could give these lovely chintz-covered ones, adorned with fragrant piggy sachets, for presents, or keep them to add a floral touch to your own wardrobe. The smooth, unruched construction, large-scale chintz fabric, and overall lack of fussiness make the hangers look chic and fresh. They would also look good in a small-scale novelty pig print.

CUTTING OUT THE HANGER

1 Find the bias of the piece of fabric by folding it diagonally at one end, so that the crosswise grain is parallel to the selvage. Mark this diagonal fold line with chalk or pins; this is the true bias. Now draw another line, parallel to it and 8 inches away. Cut out a 20 inch length of this bias strip.

MAKING THE HANGER

2 Bind around the hook of the hanger with narrow ribbon, beginning with a blob of fabric adhesive and binding tightly. Knot the ribbon at the base of the hook.

3 Cut 1¼ inch wide strips of batting, and wrap around the hanger. Bind over again in the opposite direction, until the hanger is really fat.

4 Fold the fabric in half crosswise and then in half lengthwise. Snip across the central folded corner to make a tiny hole exactly in the middle of the fabric. Slide the hook through this hole and pin fabric to batting across the top of the hanger.

5 Pin the fabric together along the base of the hanger, turning under the raw edges as you go and trimming off any excess fabric. Slipstitch together.

CUTTING OUT THE SACHET

6 Cut the felt in half to make two 4¾ x 3½ inch rectangles.

7 Using the pattern on page 119, trace off the pig outline onto tissue paper. Lay the tissue paper pig in the center of one felt rectangle, and carefully cut out only the oval.

8 Cut out one rectangle of net the same size as a felt rectangle.

MAKING THE SACHET

9 Pin the cut-out piece of felt over the net and over the remaining piece of felt, matching the outer edges. Lift one end and insert a small amount of potpourri between the net and the bottom piece of felt.

10 Carefully stitch all around, following the pig outline on the tissue paper. Tear off the tissue paper and then stitch around the central oval. Cut around the pig with pinking shears, through all three layers.

11 Tie a length of narrow ribbon around the neck of the hanger. Hand sew the pig to the ends of the ribbon.

12 Tie a length of wider ribbon around the neck of the hanger and into a neat bow. Trim all the ribbon ends diagonally.

MATERIALS

For one hanger and sachet:

- 20 x 8 inch piece of chintz fabric cut on the bias (see method)
- Matching threads
- Wooden coathanger
- Narrow ribbon, for binding hook
- Fabric adhesive
- Thick batting
- Tissue paper
- 7 x 5 inch piece of felt
- Scrap of net
- Small amount of potpourri
- Ribbons
- Pinking shears

PERKY PIG

This charming picture of a perky, though slightly bemused, porker would look perfect in a child's nursery — or, for that matter, anywhere in the house. Naive appliqué designs are now more popular than ever. The farmyard and nature are, of course, among the main sources of inspiration for naive motifs since bright colors and appealing animals are perfect for a stylized treatment. The beauty of naive designs is that simple, childlike (and easy to draw!) shapes really come into their own.

Finished size 10 x 7 inches

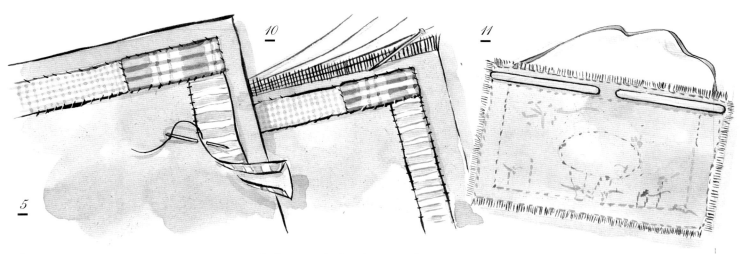

CUTTING OUT

1 Using the patterns on page 120, cut out the pig's body and head from the white polkadot fabric, and the legs from the black polkadot fabric.

2 From the black polkadot fabric, cut out crude circles for the large spots, and rough squares for the ears. From the pink fabric cut a ⅜ inch circle for the snout.

3 Cut out 1⅜ inch wide strips of fabric for the border.

APPLIQUÉ

4 Press under ¼ inch on all edges except those that will be covered (ie tops of legs and bottoms of ears). All the edges of each border strip should be turned under by this same amount.

5 Position the border strips about ⅜ inch in from the edge of the linen. These will serve as a frame. Pin and then blindstitch or slipstitch in place, using colored sewing thread that will contrast with the fabrics. The stitching is part of the design.

6 Pin the pig's body and then its head in place. Stick the ends of the ears underneath the top of its head, and the ends of the legs under its belly, with the other ends overlapping the border. If desired, slip a little batting under the head and body, to create a hint of three dimensions. Blindstitch or slipstitch these in place. As you sew, check that all the seam allowances are completely turned under.

7 Pin on the big black spots and the pink snout, and sew in place.

8 In addition to (or instead of) blindstitch or slipstitch, you could use a small running stitch to secure the appliquéd pieces.

EMBROIDERY

9 Embroider French knots for the pig's eyes, and chain stitch a curly tail, both in pink embroidery floss. With satin stitch embroider a blackbird on the pig's back, making a yellow beak using straight stitch. Work a yellow sun in straight stitch, and flying blackbirds also in straight stitch. Use satin stitch and French knots in various colors for the flowers, and backstitch in green or brown for the stems. Finally, add a smile with backstitch in light pink.

FINISHING

10 Make a self-fringe by using a pin to carefully remove to a depth of ⅜ inch the threads running parallel to each edge.

11 Glue the two popsickle sticks to the back of the picture. Sew the ends of the ribbon to the front of the picture at the top. On top, sew ribbon bows.

MATERIALS

- Scraps of lightweight cotton fabrics in polkadot, checked, striped. and floral patterns, and in plain pink for snout
- 10 x 7 inch piece of natural-colored linen
- Sewing thread to match linen and to contrast with cotton fabrics
- Embroidery floss in black, pink, yellow, and green, plus a selection of other colors for flowers
- Batting
- 24 inch length of narrow ribbon
- Two flat wooden popsickle sticks

THIS LITTLE PIGGY

Whenever you want to go to market, take this snappy tote bag with you. Despite its stylish looks and sturdy construction, it's easy to make. The pig motifs have been cut out from a "farmyard"-design fabric and stitched onto canvas, so if the pig fabric you use is not similar, you may have to position the motifs differently, or change the dimensions of the bag. Rectangular motifs work well with the straight lines of the design and fabric. Nevertheless, the basic bag will be suitable for a wide variety of designs.

Finished size 18 x 12¾ inches excluding straps

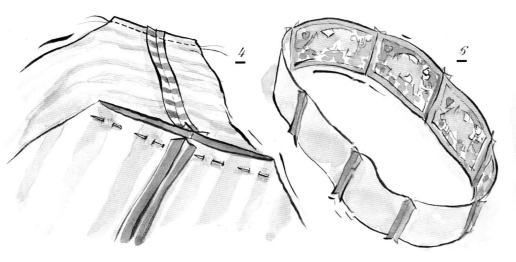

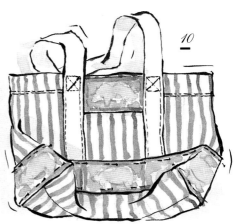

CUTTING OUT

1 Using the pattern on page 122, cut two pieces from striped fabric.

2 Cut out ten pig motifs, leaving an allowance of ⅜ inch all around.

MAKING THE BAG

3 Place the two bag pieces with right sides together and raw edges even. Pin and stitch the side seams and the base seam, taking a ¾ inch seam allowance. At this stage, do not stitch the L-shaped section between these.

4 Now bring the sides of the bag around over the base, matching the seams. Pin and stitch across the ends, forming the bag base, which will be approximately 4½ inches wide.

5 Turn under and press 2 inches along the top edge, then repeat to form a double hem. Pin and stitch.

ATTACHING THE PIG MOTIFS

6 The dimensions of this bag were designed for this particular motif, so eight motifs will fit exactly around the base of the bag. Pin and stitch them into a ring, right sides together, and taking ⅜ inch seams. Trim the seams and press them open.

7 Turn under the seam allowances at the top and base edges of the motif ring. Pin and baste them in place. Pin the ring around the base edge of the bag, but do not stitch it in place yet.

8 Turn under the seam allowances on the remaining two motifs, and baste these in place on each side of the bag, just down from the top edge, and centered between the side seams. Stitch in place around all four edges.

MAKING THE HANDLES

9 Cut the length of webbing in half. Lay one of these lengths on one side of the bag, arranging it on either side of the central motif to form handles. Tuck the raw ends of the webbing under the motif ring around the base of the bag.

10 Pin and stitch the webbing in place, stitching a cross at the top of each handle for strength. Stitch a handle to the other side of the bag in the same way.

11 Stitch the motif ring in position around the base of the bag, stitching along both the bottom edge of the ring and the top edge, and stitching through the handle ends at the same time to secure them.

12 If desired, cut a piece of cardboard to fit the base of the bag. Cover it with a "sleeve" made from the remaining strip of striped fabric. Place inside the bag.

MATERIALS

- 43 x 20 inch piece of striped sturdy fabric such as canvas
- Fabric with rectangular pig motifs – these are approximately 4½ x 3¾ inches
- 2¾ yards webbing 1½ inches wide
- Sewing thread to match
- Thick cardboard

A NEW TWIST

Give a traditionally styled kimono a new twist with these curly-tailed porkers. The tails are made from narrow ribbon twisted into a coil and sewn under the appliquéd pig shapes. For the most dramatic look, choose vivid colors for the pigs and apples, and a contrasting (and non-directional) fabric for the kimono. Here, the motifs are added to the front only, but they could be applied all the way around the lower hem and sleeve edge (in which case you'll need extra fabric and ribbon for them).

Finished length (shoulder to hem) 42¼ inches

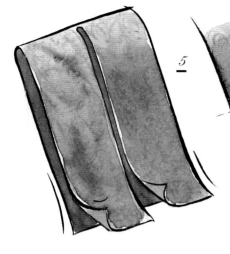

CUTTING OUT

1 Cut out the following pieces from fabric: one kimono body 88 x 28 inches, two sleeves 25 x 10 inches, two pockets 10 x 7 inches, one belt 72 x 5 inches.

2 Cut two rectangles, each 2 x 3½ inches for the belt loops.

3 Cut two 2 inch wide bias strips (page 106), each 50 inches long.

4 Cut a piece of interfacing using the belt pattern.

5 To create the front opening, fold the kimono body in half crosswise; press the fold, then open it out flat. Now fold the kimono body in half lengthwise and press a fold in the front half only (ie to one side of the crosswise fold, which corresponds to the shoulder line). Unfold, and cut along this center front line as far as the crosswise fold.

6 To make the neck opening, mark points on the crosswise fold 2¼ inches from the center on each side. In addition, mark a point on the back half which is 1 inch from the intersection point of the center front opening and crosswise fold. Finally, mark on the center front opening a point 10 inches from the intersection point. Connect the points you have marked with a smooth line, and cut around the line to make the neck opening.

POCKETS

7 For each pocket, finish all pocket edges, then, with right sides together, turn under 1½ inches on one short edge. Stitch this self-facing to the pocket along the side edges. Trim and turn right side out.

8 Turn under the remaining edges of the pocket and press. Topstitch 1 inch from the top edge.

9 With the faced edge at the top, position the pockets (right side facing up) on the right side of the kimono front, centering each between the side edge and the center front opening. The bottom edges should be 15 inches from the bottom raw edge of the kimono. Topstitch close to the outer edges of the pocket, leaving the top edge open (see Tips).

KIMONO SEAMS

10 Staystitch the edge of the neck opening (see Tips).

MATERIALS

- 2½ yards black cotton fabric 45 inches wide
- 1¼ yards pink cotton fabric 45 inches wide
- 3 x 5 inch piece of red cotton fabric
- 2 yards pink double-faced satin ribbon ⅛ inch wide
- ½ yard green satin ribbon ⅝ inch wide
- Sewing thread to match
- Interfacing, for belt
- Fusible web

NOTE

All seam allowances are ⅝ inch unless stated otherwise.

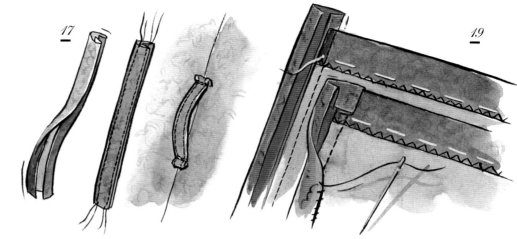

11 On the seamline of one long edge of a sleeve, mark the center. With right sides together and raw edges even, match this to the crosswise fold in the kimono front. Stitch along the seamline for the entire length of the sleeve, then finish the raw edges of the seam. Repeat for the other sleeve.

12 With right sides together and raw edges even, join the kimono side seams from the bottom edge to the sleeve seam. Finish the raw edges.

13 With right sides together and raw edges even, stitch each underarm sleeve seam. Finish the raw edges.

14 Finish the raw bottom edges of the sleeves and kimono. Turn under and press a 1¼ inch hem on the sleeves and a 1¾ inch hem on the kimono body. Topstitch the hems.

BELT AND BELT LOOPS

15 Apply the interfacing to the wrong side of the belt. With right sides together and raw edges even, stitch the long edges. Turn right side out and press flat. Trim the short edges even.

16 With wrong sides together, fold each belt loop lengthwise so the raw edges meet in the center. Press. Now fold this in half lengthwise and press. Topstitch along both folds.

17 Turn under ⅜ inch at each end of the belt loops. Position the loops at the side seams of the kimono, about 7½ inches down from the underarm seams. Stitch in place across the folded top and bottom edges of each loop.

BINDING

18 Join the two bias strips to make one continuous strip, then press two folds into it along the long edges (see page 106). Open out the folds.

19 With right sides together and raw edges even, pin and stitch the bias binding to the neck and front edges of the kimono. Leave an extra ½ inch of bias binding at both ends at the hem. Fold up and pin the bias binding extensions at the hemline. Wrap the binding over to the wrong side and slipstitch the folded edge to the hemline.

APPLIQUE

20 Following the manufacturer's instructions, iron enough fusible web to the wrong side of the pink fabric to make 16 pigs from the pig pattern on page 120. Transfer eight of these pig shapes to the paper backing. Now transfer eight more that are the mirror image of the first eight. Cut out, then remove the paper backing.

21 Repeat the procedure in step 20 for the red fabric, using the apple pattern on page 120.

TIPS

• Pockets often get a lot of wear, so to help prevent them from gradually coming away from the kimono body, reinforce the stitching at the top by backstitching to form a little triangle when attaching pockets to the garment.

• Staystitching will help prevent a curved edge such as a neckline from stretching while you are handling it or stitching the seam. It also serves as a useful guideline when you have to clip curves within

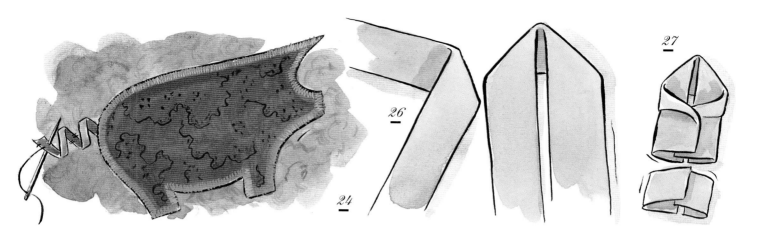

22 Fuse the pig appliqués to each sleeve edge at the front, positioning them 1½ inches from the hemmed edge. Arrange the pigs in pairs facing each other, allowing 1½ inches between snouts.

23 Fuse pairs of pigs to the lower kimono edge at the front, again allowing 1½ inches between snouts but positioning them 2 inches from the hemmed edge.

24 Pin 5 inches of pink ribbon behind each pig for a tail. Machine satin stitch all edges of the pigs. Coil the ribbon around a pencil, remove the pencil, and tack the end of the ribbon in place with a few stitches.

25 Sandwich each end of the belt between two pigs, and machine satin stitch all edges of the pigs. Knot and sew ribbon tails to these pigs.

26 Each pair of pigs on the kimono (but not on the belt) has an apple, and each apple has a leaf. To make a leaf, cut a 3 inch length of green ribbon. Holding the ribbon horizontally with the wrong side facing you, make a diagonal fold in one half so it is at right angles to the other half. Do the same for the other half, so that the ends of the ribbon are even at the bottom and a triangle is formed on the back at the top.

27 Now fold the ribbon into thirds so that the outside edges overlap. Trim off the bottom to leave a ½ inch base. Pin or baste the ribbon leaf together to hold.

28 Pin a ribbon leaf behind an apple at the top. Fuse an apple between each pair of pigs. Machine satin stitch all edges of the apples.

a seam allowance. To staystitch, simply machine stitch through one layer only, ⅛ inch inside the seamline (ie, within the seam allowance).

THAT DARNED PIG

All the decoration (apart from the ribbon) on this colorful sweater has been embroidered, mainly with duplicate stitch. This technique, also known as Swiss darning, enables you to turn plain knitted garments into beautiful and intricate picture sweaters with very little needleworking skill — and you don't even have to know how to knit! The only requirement is that the part of the garment being decorated must be knitted in stockinette stitch. Other forms of embroidery can be worked on garter- and moss- stitched knitting as well as on stockinette.

MATERIALS

- Sport yarn weight sweater with a stockinette stitch gauge of 22 stitches and 23 rows to 4 inches
- Small amounts of sport

yarn in:

A — light pink

B — dark pink

C — emerald

D — red

E — yellow

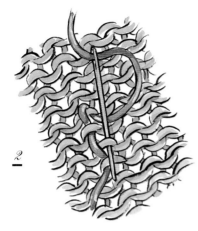

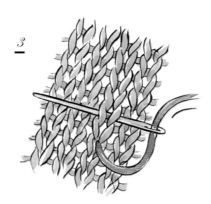

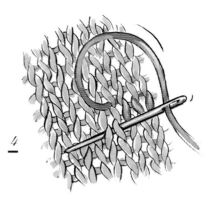

USING A CHART

1 In an embroidery chart, each square represents a stitch. The symbols or colors in the squares indicate the colors of embroidery floss or yarn used, and sometimes also the stitches. For duplicate stitch, the grid represents the background of stockinette stitch. On the chart on pages 80–1, locate the center front (marked as two squares with diagonal lines in them). This is about 4 inches above the top of the waistband and is your starting point.

DUPLICATE STITCH

2 Thread the needle with the dark pink yarn, and secure it at the back with a couple of stitches.

3 Bring the needle through from back to front at the base of the stitch to be covered. Insert it under the stitch above, taking the needle from right to left. Now insert it from front to back through the base of the first stitch.

4 Carry on in this way, covering the stitches as shown on the chart, and changing to light pink (or green, for the eye), as necessary. Be careful not to pull the yarn too tight – the gauge needs to match that of the sweater so that it will not pucker.

OTHER EMBROIDERY

5 For the grass the pig is standing in, cut 2¼ inch lengths of emerald yarn (C). With the crochet hook, fold two lengths of yarn in half together. With the right side of the work facing you, insert the hook horizontally through the knit fabric. Place the two loops of yarn over the hook and draw them through the work. Place the ends of the yarn over the hook, and draw them through the loops in the hook. Pull up tightly to secure. Repeat over the grass area shown on the chart. Trim the tufts to ¼ inch.

6 For the flowers on the sleeves and above the waistband, work lazy daisy stitch (see page 111), in red or yellow, with green leaves and stems.

- *10 inch length of ¼ inch wide red satin ribbon*
- *Darning needle or tapestry needle*
- *Medium crochet hook*
- *Sewing thread to match light pink yarn (A) and red ribbon*

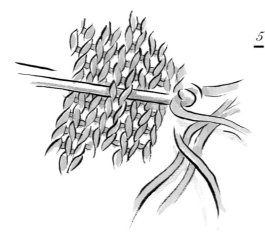

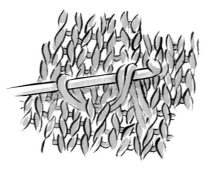

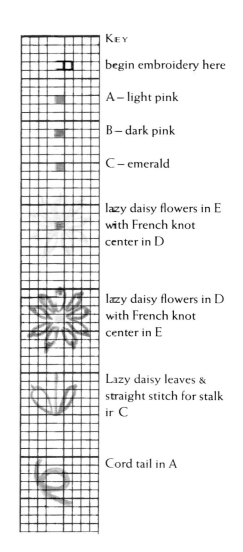

7 For the center of each flower, work a French knot (see page 110), in yellow or red (to contrast with the "petals").

8 For the decoration around the neck, work cross-stitches (see page 110) in red.

FINISHING

9 Cut a 7 inch length of light pink yarn (A) and fold it in half. Place it around a knitting needle. Holding one end in each hand, twist the ends together. Without letting go of the ends, hold them taut and fold them in half again. Let go of the folded end and allow it to coil. Take it off the needle and knot the loose ends together. Smooth it down from the knotted end to even out the twists. Trim the loose ends to ¼ inch.

10 Attach the folded end to the back of the pig. Loop the tail around the areas shown on the chart and slipstitch the free end in place.

11 Tie the ribbon where indicated on the chart and slipstitch it in position.

KEY

begin embroidery here

A – light pink

B – dark pink

C – emerald

lazy daisy flowers in E with French knot center in D

lazy daisy flowers in D with French knot center in E

Lazy daisy leaves & straight stitch for stalk ir C

Cord tail in A

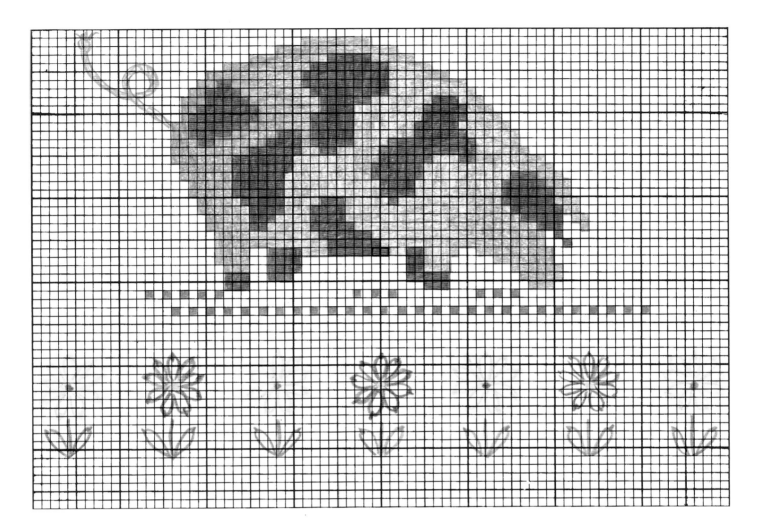

FLIGHTS OF FANCY

These fantastical flying pigs form an unusual set comprising a pair of earrings and a brooch. They are made using machine embroidery and gold metallic thread. Separate layers of muslin are completely covered with stitching and then glued together to form each pig. The technique does require some practice, but a special sewing machine that does automatic embroidery stitches is not necessary. Once you get used to the technique of "free embroidery," all sorts of unusual and dramatic effects are possible.

Finished size of brooch
6 1/4 x 3 inches

Finished size of earrings
3 x 1 3/4 inches

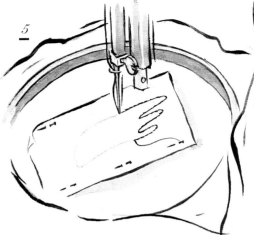

PREPARATION

1 Cut pieces of muslin large enough to fit in your embroidery hoop.

2 Using the patterns on pages 120–1, trace the designs onto tracing paper. The wings are made up of three tiers, which must be done separately. There are six tiers (three per side) for each earring or brooch.

3 Following the directions on page 109, prepare the sewing machine for free embroidery and place a piece of muslin in the embroidery hoop. Thread the machine with dark embroidery thread.

4 Pin the tracing paper to the muslin.

EMBROIDERING THE WINGS

5 Stitch the outline of each tier through both tracing paper and muslin. Do not place them too close together; you will need several pieces of muslin for each brooch/earring.

6 Carefully cut away the tracing paper, leaving the stitched outlines.

7 Thread the machine with gold metallic thread. Starting from the center and working outward (to reduce puckering), fill in the outline using a free running stitch, as though you were using color crayons. Adjust the tension if necessary.

EMBROIDERING THE HEAD

8 Stitch the outline of the head on the muslin in the same way as for the wings (steps 4–6), again using the dark thread.

9 Fill in the features with gently curving lines of free running stitch, following the contours of the face, rather like the contour lines of a topographic map.

10 Use tiny pieces of muslin to pad the cheeks, snout, and forehead, embroidering densely over them and cutting away excess.

11 Darker colors should be used for shadows and lines, and lighter colors for highlights.

12 Embroider the eyes, nostrils, and mouth with a dark brown thread.

ASSEMBLING THE PIGS

13 With the muslin still in the hoop, apply a layer of white glue to the front and back of each embroidered piece, and allow to dry.

14 Remove the muslin from the hoop and cut out each piece carefully, as close to the embroidery as possible.

15 Glue the three left-hand wing tiers together, applying glue only to the top center, as shown. Position the smallest on top and the largest on the bottom, fanning out the feathered ends with your fingers. Do the same for the right-hand tiers. Allow to dry.

16 Glue the top of the wings to each side of the back of the head, and allow to dry completely.

17 For a brooch, glue the fastening to the back. For an earring, hand sew the fastening to the top of the head.

MATERIALS

- *Tracing paper*
- *Muslin*
- *8–9 inch embroidery hoop*
- *Machine embroidery thread in dark color for* *outlining and in various colors for faces, from cream through pinks to gray and brown*
- *Gold metallic machine embroidery thread*
- *White glue*
- *Brooch pin*
- *Pair of drop-earring fastenings*

NOTE

Remember always to keep your fingers away from the needle, as there is no presser foot.

PIGS
FOR
KIDS

Whose little pigs are these, these, these?

Whose little pigs are these?

They are Roger the Cook's, I know

by their looks;

I found them among my peas.

Traditional

UP FRONT

This jaunty fellow just knows he will make an awesome addition to the front of any T-shirt. After all, this is a pig with attitude. To add him to your T-shirt, or give him as a gift, all you have to do is trace the design at the back of the book then color him in using a selection of bright fabric paints and a paintbrush — it's the perfect opportunity to try out the wide range of fabric paints now available, without actually being able to draw.

MATERIALS

- White cotton T-shirt
- Fabric paints suitable for natural fibers, including gold and silver
- Paintbrush

PREPARATION

1 Wash and iron the T-shirt if it is new. Most cottons have special finishes, which make them less receptive to dyes and fabric paints and which will therefore need to be washed out.

2 Experiment with the fabric paints on a fabric remnant, ideally an old cotton T-shirt similar to this one. This will help you to become familiar with the paints and the brush. It is particularly important to play around with mixes for shadowy areas and lighter areas. Do not use black to darken your colors as it will produce a muddy result. Try touches of dark red, dark blue, or brown.

3 Place a large piece of cardboard inside the T-shirt. To prevent the fabric from stretching, moving around, or wrinkling as you work, tape the T-shirt to the table with masking tape.

4 Transfer the design on page 126 onto the T-shirt using the "shading" method (page 112). (The design is already reversed, so that it will be the right way around on the T-shirt.)

PAINTING

5 Using a nylon artist's brush, fill in the outlines.

6 Mix the colored paints with white paint where highlights (the lightest parts) are needed. For the shadowy areas, make up a suitable mix, or use a deeper shade of your color.

FINISHING

7 If you are using paints that require "fixing," place a piece of cotton over the painting and iron for about two minutes.

PREPARE TO PIG OUT

These parent-and-child aprons are just what you need when you, and any helpers, are preparing a feast. The galloping gourmets on the pockets are sure to make it a runaway success! First, the colors are painted onto the design on the fabric, then the black is printed with a lino block. Instructions are given for making the aprons, which are very quick and easy to sew, but if you prefer, you could use readymade cotton aprons. Because the fabric paints are "fixed," the aprons are washable.

Finished size adult's 34 inches wide x 29½ inches long; child's 14½ inches wide x 19 inches long

MATERIALS

- Ticking 36 inches wide: adult's 1 yard; child's ⅔ yard
- Black twill tape 1 inch wide: adult's 2½ yards; child's 1⅜ yards
- White or off-white 100% cotton, 36 inches wide: adult's ⅓ yard; child's ¼ yard
- Sewing thread to match
- Printmaking lino block:

CUTTING OUT THE APRON

1 The aprons will fit an average-sized adult, or a young child, but can easily be made smaller or larger. Using either the adult's or the child's pattern on page 125, cut out one apron piece from ticking. (Do not cut out the pocket at this stage.)

2 Cut a 19 inch length of twill tape for the adult neck tie, or a 16 inch length for the child's neck tie. Cut the remaining tape in half to use for the two waist ties. These are long enough to wrap around the back and then tie at the front.

SEWING THE APRON

3 Position the ends of the neck tie on the wrong side of the apron at each side of the top edge, with raw edges even. Adjust to fit if necessary, and make sure that the tie isn't twisted, then baste in place.

4 Position one end of each of the two waist ties on the wrong side of the apron on the curved edges at each side, with raw edges even. Baste in place.

5 Turn and press a double ⅜ inch seam on the top edge, both curved edges, and both side edges. Stitch near the turned-under edge of each, stitching through the ties as well.

6 Remove the basting, press the ties in the opposite direction, and stitch each seam again, this time stitching near the outer edge, and once again stitching through the ties. (Be sure to check that they are at right angles to the seam as you stitch.)

7 At the bottom edge, turn under and press ⅜ inch and then a further 1 inch. Stitch.

PREPARING THE POCKET FABRIC

8 Wash and iron the pocket fabric, as this will allow it to take the paints more successfully.

9 Cut the pocket fabric into a rectangle measuring 18 x 10 inches for the adult's apron, or 13 x 8 inches for the child's.

CUTTING THE LINO BLOCK

10 Wash the lino block in warm, soapy water in order to remove any grease. Leave to dry.

11 Enlarge the design on page 115 by 200 per cent for the adult's and by 145 per cent for the child's pocket. Trace the enlarged design. Now use carbon paper to transfer all the deail of the tracing, *in reverse* (in other words, using the back of the tracing so that the image is the wrong way around), to the cutting surface of the lino. Go over the image on the lino with a permanent marker pen.

adult's 9⅞ x 6¹/₁₆ inches; child's 7⁹/₁₆ x 4⁷/₁₆ inches

• *Tracing paper*
• *Carbon paper*
• *Permanent marker (non*

water-based), in black
• *Lino-cutting tools (see page 91)*
• *Fine-grade sandpaper*
• *Masking tape*
• *Fabric paints (see Tips),*

1 ounce size, in two bright colors and black
• *Paintbrushes (see Tips)*

12 Before beginning to cut, practice using the cutting tools on a small piece of scrap lino. Always remember to cut away from your body, and away from the hand holding the lino. To cut, hold the cutting tool with the "V" or "U" turned upward, and push it forward gently to make a groove. To create a curved line, turn the block as you go.

13 Once you have become familiar with the tools and the effects you can create, begin cutting out the areas around the outline to make the design stand out in relief. Remember that anything that is not cut away will print. The background texture is achieved by cutting carefully but randomly away at the area between the pig and the border.

14 When you have finished cutting, gently sand the surface with fine-grade sandpaper, to make sure that there are no loose bits left on the block, which would spoil the effect. Wipe off any dust and put the block to one side while you paint the color onto the fabric.

PAINTING THE FABRIC

15 Place your tracing of the design, the *right way around*, on the back of the carbon paper, and tape both to the center of the rectangle of pocket fabric, using masking tape. Transfer the outline of the pig and the outer straight edge of the border to the fabric by drawing over them with a pencil.

16 Mask out the edge of the border with strips of masking tape. This will help keep the fabric around the image clean and will also help to register (align) the lino printing block with the color background.

17 Using one of the bright-colored paints, and one of the small brushes, paint in the pig. Make sure that the whole pig has an even coating of paint – it can be thinned with a small amount of water if necessary.

18 Now paint the area around the pig in the other bright color, using the second small brush, and taking the paint right up to the masking tape.

19 Allow the paint to dry naturally then fix it as directed by the manufacturer. For example, the directions may say to iron with a hot iron on the reverse side and then on the right side for approximately four minutes.

BLOCK PRINTING

20 Using the medium-sized brush, carefully paint an even amount of black paint onto the surface of the lino block, taking care not to saturate the lino with paint.

TIPS

● To make the lino block easier to cut, warm it under hot water for a few minutes.

● Do not allow children to be involved in cutting the lino block, or even to handle the tools.

● You will need one medium-sized and two small stiff flat-backed brushes. Oil-painting brushes work well, or any type made of bristle or – appropriately – hog's hair.

● The fabric paints must be soft, water-based, and non-toxic.

21 Place the pocket fabric right side up on some newspaper. Taking care to line up the edges of the block with the edges of your painted design – and making sure that you're not printing upside-down! – carefully place the inked block face down on the painted area of fabric.

22 Apply pressure to the back of the block using your hand or a roller. Now carefully lift the fabric and block, holding them together. Flip them over so that the fabric is on top. Rub the back of the fabric gently.

23 Lift one end of the fabric to check that the paint has taken. If it hasn't, apply a little more paint to the lino surface, then replace the fabric and apply pressure with your hand. Do the same at the other end.

24 When you are satisfied with the result, slowly and carefully lift the fabric off the lino block. Allow the paint to dry naturally, then fix with an iron as in step 19. Finally, iron the whole rectangle.

MAKING THE POCKET

25 Using either the adult's or the child's pocket pattern on page 125, cut out the pocket from the block-printed rectangle, insuring that the design is positioned centrally.

26 Turn under ⅜ inch on all edges of the pocket, clipping the curves within the seam allowances so that the fabric will lie flat; press. Turn under and press a further ⅜ inch along the top edge and stitch this double hem.

27 Use the placement lines on the pattern to position the pocket on the apron front. Pin and stitch the pocket to the apron close to the curved edge.

28 To prevent the relatively wide pocket on the adult's apron from gaping open, hand sew it invisibly to the apron about ⅜ inch down from the top edge, in the center.

THE CUTTING EDGE

Lino-cutting tools are widely available, individually and as kits. The lino blocks are cut to size with a craft knife, then the design is cut with gouging tools, which make V- or U-shaped grooves. For a beginner, a small and a medium-sized V-shaped cutter and a small and a fairly large U-shaped cutter are useful. Very broad U-shaped (semi-circular) cutters are good for removing large areas. An oilstone is needed for sharpening the tools; a very narrow oilstone is called a slip.

PIG HEADED

Colorful embroidered detailing on a collar and cuffs will transform a plain ready-made garment into something special. Designed to fit the space, each piggy portrait in its heart "frame" nestles neatly into the shape of the collar, while a full-length fellow comfortably fills a large part of each cuff. Both designs are worked using "waste canvas," which enables you to embroider on fabrics where it would otherwise be impossible. To complete the detailing of the shirt, the pig theme is carried one step further, with tiny pig's head buttons.

Finished size of embroidery on each side of collar 2 x 2¼ inches

Finished size of embroidery on cuff 1¼ x 2¾ inches

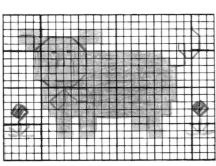
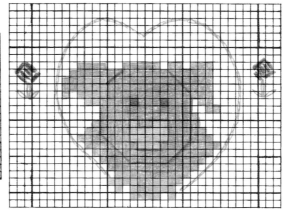
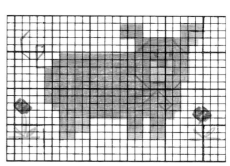

CUTTING OUT AND PREPARATION

1 For each side of the collar, cut a 2¾ x 2½ inch piece of waste canvas.

2 For each cuff, cut a 3 x 1½ inch piece of waste canvas.

3 To find the middle of each piece of waste canvas, fold it in half lengthwise. Center it on the collar or cuff and baste the waste canvas in position.

EMBROIDERY

4 On the chart above, each square represents one cross-stitch. Each symbol indicates the color that stitch should be. All the cross-stitches are worked using two strands of embroidery floss. (Separate the six strands, letting them untwist, and then recombine two of them.) Do not cut the floss any longer than about 12–15 inches, or it will knot and tangle. You will not need to use a hoop for such a small area.

5 Following the hand-embroidery instructions on page 108 and the Stitch Glossary on page 110, begin stitching from the center point. This is marked on the chart. Work in orange or pink (or, on the collar, deep rust for the eyes), changing color when necessary.

6 When all the cross-stitch is completed on the collar pieces, work the remaining stitches as shown on the chart: backstitch (one strand of deep rust) around the face and snout; chain stitch (two strands of blue) for the heart; bullion knots (two strands of red) for the flowers; and lazy daisy stitch (two strands of green) for the leaves/stems.

7 Similarly, for the cuffs, work backstitch (one strand of deep rust) for the tail and around the face and snout; backstitch (one strand of blue) for the bow; French knots (two strands of deep rust) for the eyes;

bullion knots (two strands of red) for the flowers; and lazy daisy stitch (two strands of green) for the leaves/stems.

FINISHING

8 Once the embroidery is finished, carefully remove the waste canvas, one thread at a time, pulling out all the threads in one direction and then all the threads in the other direction.

9 To press the embroidered collar and cuffs, first put a folded towel on the ironing board. Place the collar or cuff embroidered side down, and cover it with a damp cloth (if the shirt is dry) or a dry cloth (if the shirt is damp from being – gently – washed). Iron only very lightly.

MATERIALS

- *Shirt with suitable collar and cuffs*
- *12 x 2½ inch piece of waste canvas, 14-count*
- *Stranded embroidery floss: 4½ yards pink*
- *and 1 yard each orange, red, deep rust, green, and blue*
- *Size 24 tapestry needle*

SQUEAK, PIGGY, SQUEAK

A colorful bib featuring a petulant pig that squeaks when its nose is pressed will brighten up any baby's mealtime. Use a check gingham fabric for the wall the pig is looking over. If you can find one with flowers growing up it, so much the better, then you can match some of the flower colors to the main fabric and binding, and to the pig. Striped fabric would also be suitable. The pig's face is embroidered, but you could use fabric paints or appliquéd features.

Finished size 12 x 14 inches

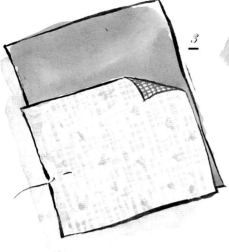

CUTTING OUT

1 From the main fabric cut two 14 x 12 inch pieces, cutting them along one selvage edge in order to leave enough for the binding.

2 From the gingham cut one 10 x 12 inch piece for the wall.

MAKING THE BIB

3 Place the gingham rectangle on top of one of the fabric rectangles, with right sides together, matching the 12 inch edges. Mark a line 5 inches in from this edge and stitch along this line. Press.

4 Fold the gingham in half along the stitching line, wrong sides together and matching raw edges. Baste all three layers together around the edges.

5 Using a scrap of the main fabric, enclose the squeaker in a small stitched bag about 2 inches square. Hand sew this onto the back of the bib where the snout will be.

MAKING THE HEAD

6 Using transfer pencil and paper, trace the head and features from the pattern on page 120. Iron this onto the pink sateen.

7 Embroider the pig's features on the pink sateen using two strands of dark gray embroidery floss and stem stitch (see page 111). Work its eyes in satin stitch using the dark gray floss and highlighting each with white sewing thread.

8 Cut out the pig's head. Pin the head onto the bib, checking that the snout is over the squeaker. Turn the raw edges under by 3/8 inch, and slipstitch the pig onto the bib, carefully snipping into the seam allowance at the corners and on curves.

FINISHING THE BIB

9 With wrong sides together, pin the other main fabric rectangle to the back of the bib and baste around the bottom and side edges.

10 Cut out the neck of the bib using part of a 6 inch saucer as a template. Cut off the corners of the bib, rounding each off smoothly.

BINDING THE EDGES

11 Cut 1¾ inch wide strips of bias binding (see page 106) and join them to make a strip 68 inches long.

12 With wrong sides together, fold the long raw edges of the strip in to meet in the center; press. Open out the folds. With right sides together, pin the binding around the neck edge, and stitch along the fold line. Wrap binding over to the wrong side; slipstitch the folded edge to the seamline.

13 Attach binding all around the raw edges, as in step 12. Leave an extra 12 inches at each side of the neck edge, and stitch up these ties, tucking in the raw ends to neaten.

14 Remove any basting that shows. Press the bib, avoiding the squeaker.

MATERIALS

- ½ yard cotton, for main fabric and binding
- ¼ yard gingham, for "wall"
- 8 x 7 inch piece of pink sateen or cotton, for pig's face
- Sewing thread to match and in white
- Flat waterproof squeaker about 1¾ inches in diameter
- Dark gray stranded embroidery floss
- Transfer pencil and paper

FROM HEAD TO TAIL

A sow and her two piglets — plus close-up "snapshots" of them — decorate this delightful crib quilt. Any baby would love having it in the crib and it would also make a good activity mat for playing on the floor. The matching wallhanging, featuring the "snapshots" without the central panel, is made in the same way. The appliqué and the quilting are both done the quick way — by machine.

Finished size of quilt
29 x 43 inches

Finished size of
wallhanging
12 x 29 inches

MATERIALS

FOR THE QUILT

- Four 7 inch squares of dark blue lightweight cotton

- Two 7 inch squares of mid blue lightweight

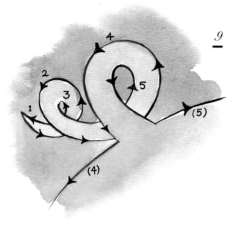

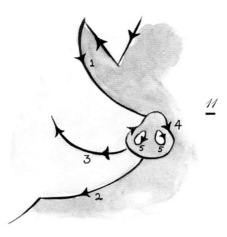

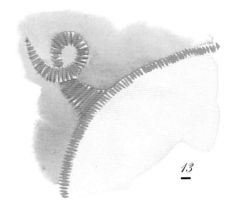

CUTTING OUT THE QUILT

1 Make paper templates from the patterns on page 123 and use these to cut out the appliqué shapes from the fabric.

2 From the pink polkadot fabric cut out one sow, four pigs' tails (of which two are in reverse), and two pigs' snouts (of which one is in reverse).

3 From the plain pink fabric cut two piglets (of which one is in reverse) and two pigs' faces (of which one is in reverse) including nostrils.

4 From the scraps of fabric cut out two black eyes and two of each of the tufts of grass in green.

5 From one floral fabric cut 2 inch wide strips on the straight grain for binding. Cut and join enough strips to make 13 feet of binding.

6 From the same floral fabric cut two 3½ x 38 inch border strips and two 3½ x 29 inch border strips.

7 From the other floral fabric cut out four 3½ x 7 inch joining strips and two 3½ x 24 inch joining strips.

APPLIQUÉING THE SQUARES

8 Pin each tail to a dark blue square, with the two straight edges even with the bottom edge and one side edge of the square. Machine baste around the shape very close to the edge; this will be covered by the machine embroidery.

9 Now machine satin stitch (page 109) around the edge. So that the tail looks as though it is curling back on itself, sew it in five short stretches as shown. Always pull the threads to the back and tie.

10 Pin each face to a mid blue square, with the two straight edges even with the top edge and one side of the square. Machine baste close to the edge of the face.

11 Machine satin stitch the outline and the smile as in step 9, tapering to a point by moving the stitch-width lever while stitching. In the same way, pin and baste the pink polkadot snout in place, and satin stitch around the edge. Add the plain pink nostrils, and satin stitch around the edge of each. Now appliqué the eye in the same way.

APPLIQUÉING THE CENTER PANEL

12 Lay the background fabric for the center panel on a flat surface. (The larger dimension goes from side to side.) Pin the sow and two piglets in position.

13 Machine baste, then machine satin stitch. Do the far legs first, next the far ears, then the near legs and belly, and finally the whole body. The piglets' tails are done as a tapering satin stitch.

14 Pin, machine baste, and satin stitch the four tufts of grass in place.

cotton
- 21 x 24 inch piece of lightweight cotton
- ¼ yard each of plain pink and pink polkadot lightweight cotton 36

inches wide
- Scraps of black cotton and green cotton
- ½ yard each of two lightweight floral-print cotton fabrics 45 inches

wide
- 32 x 48 inches backing fabric
- 32 x 48 inches lightweight batting
- Sewing thread

PIECING THE QUILT

15 Press the pieces well. All the seams will be stitched in the same way – with right sides together and raw edges even, using a straight machine stitch and taking a ½ inch seam. The seam allowances are then pressed to one side.

16 First stitch one of the short joining strips to the "pig" side of one of the tail squares.

17 Stitch the other side of the joining strip to a face square.

18 Stitch a second short joining strip to the other side of the face square.

19 Stitch a mirror-image tail square to the other side of that joining strip.

20 Repeat steps 16–19 for all short joining strips and appliquéd squares.

21 In the same way, stitch a long joining strip to the bottom edge of one of these pieced strips. Stitch the other long joining strip to the top edge of the remaining pieced strip. Stitch the other side of each of the long joining strips to the top and bottom edges of the center panel.

22 Stitch one of the longer border strips to each side. Press the seams to one side.

23 Now stitch one short border strip to the top edge and the other to the bottom edge, so the ends are flush with the side edges of the other two border strips.

QUILTING

24 Lay the backing on the work surface, wrong side facing up. Lay the batting on top and then cover with the quilt top. The batting and backing should be about 2 inches bigger all around. Baste all three layers together, in a grid of lines 12 inches apart.

25 To push and pull the quilt around easily as you stitch the quilting, either use a "walking foot" on the machine or lower the feed dogs and loosen the pressure.

26 Using a medium straight stitch and starting at the center, stitch in a continuous line about ¼ inch outside the shapes, following their outline. For the joining and border strips, quilt close to the edges.

BINDING THE QUILT

27 Trim away the excess backing fabric and batting, saving the batting.

28 Pin the binding to the *back* of the quilt along one edge, right sides together. Stitch, taking a ½ inch seam. Trim off the excess binding at the ends.

29 Pull the binding over to the front of the quilt, wrapping it over the waste strips of batting and turning under the ½ inch seam allowance. Pin and then topstitch in place, covering the previous stitching. (Keep the pressure on the machine fairly slack when doing this.) Repeat for the opposite edge.

FOR THE WALLHANGING

- One 7 inch square of dark blue lightweight cotton
- Two 7 inch squares of mid blue cotton
- ¼ yard each of plain pink and polkadot pink lightweight cotton 36 inches wide
- Scraps of black cotton
- ¼ yard each of two lightweight floral-print fabrics 45 inches wide
- 33 x 16 inches backing fabric
- 33 x 16 inches lightweight batting
- Sewing thread
- 12 inches dowel

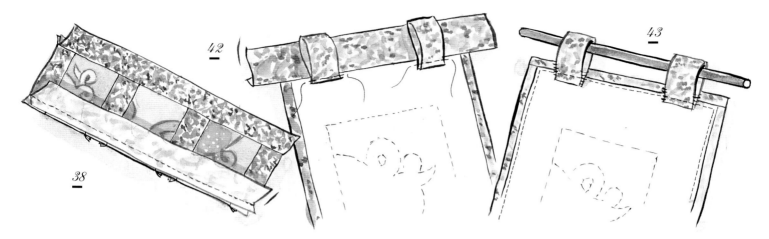

30 Bind the other two edges in the same way, but leave about 1 inch at each end. Tuck this in and stitch by hand.

CUTTING OUT THE WALLHANGING

31 From the pink polkadot fabric cut out one tail and one snout. From the plain fabric cut out one face (including nostrils) and one tail (the reverse of the spotted pink one). From the black fabric cut one eye.

32 From one floral fabric cut out 2 inch wide strips on straight grain. Join to make 7 feet of binding.

33 From the same fabric (or a different floral pattern, if you prefer) cut four joining strips, each 3½ x 7 inches.

34 From the same fabric, cut two 7 x 4 inch pieces for hanging loops.

35 From the other floral fabric, cut two 3½ x 29 inch border strips.

MAKING THE WALLHANGING

36 Appliqué the tails to the mid blue squares, and the face, snout, and nostrils to the dark blue square as for the quilt (steps 8–11).

37 With right sides together and raw edges even, stitch a joining strip to the bottom edge of a tail square, taking a ½ inch seam. Stitch another joining strip to the top of the other tail square. Stitch the other side of each of these joining strips to the top and bottom of the face square. At the top and bottom of this pieced strip, stitch the two remaining joining strips.

38 Stitch a border strip to each long edge of this pieced strip.

39 Quilt the wallhanging front to the batting and backing as for the quilt (steps 24–26).

40 Bind the two side edges and the bottom edge as for the quilt (steps 27–30). For the top edge, stitch just the first edge of the binding on the back side, so that the hanging loops can be added.

41 Fold each hanging loop piece in half lengthwise with right sides together and raw edges even. Stitch along the long edge, taking a ⅜ inch seam. Turn right side out. Press under ⅜ inch at both ends, then fold in half so these ends meet and are hidden; stitch together.

42 Pull the binding tape away from the seam, but do not wrap it around the edge yet. Position the loops 1¼ inch from the side edges of the hanging, with the stitched end that same distance from the top edge of the hanging, so that the loops project beyond the binding a little at the base. Baste near the stitched end.

43 Complete the binding of the top edge, topstitching through the ends of the hanging loops at the same time. Remove the basting and hand sew each side of the loops to the binding. Insert the dowel.

TIPS

• When basting the quilt layers together, do not knot the threads. Leaving them loose will make them easier to remove.

• You may prefer to use the appliquéd fabric double thickness if your background fabrics are in strong colors, in which case increase the amounts.

PAJAMA
PIG

Make bedtime fun with a pajama pig. Not only will children actually want to get ready for bed, they will also be more inclined to tidy away their pajamas in the morning! During the day, the pajama pig dozes appealingly on the bed, awaiting her big moment. Make no mistake, this pig is not just a pretty face — she is eager to set a good example. Her front is two layers of fabric with batting sandwiched between. Her back is the same but has an opening for the pajamas. Piping, hoofs, floppy ears, a pleated snout, embroidered eyelashes, and a curly tail all add to this pig's enormous charm.

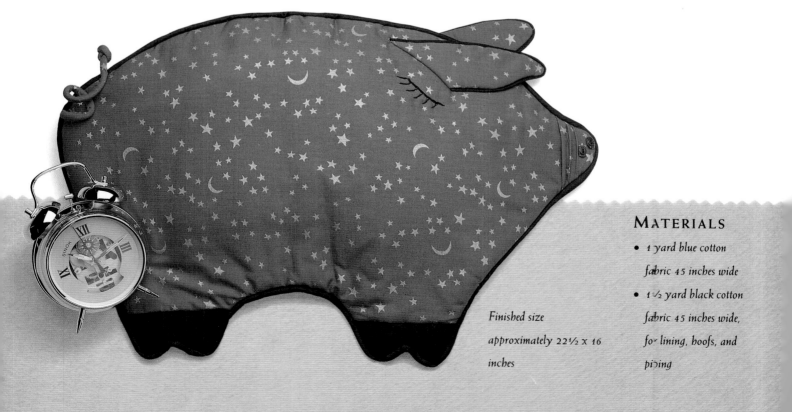

Finished size approximately 22½ x 16 inches

MATERIALS

- 1 yard blue cotton fabric 45 inches wide
- 1½ yard black cotton fabric 45 inches wide, for lining, hoofs, and piping

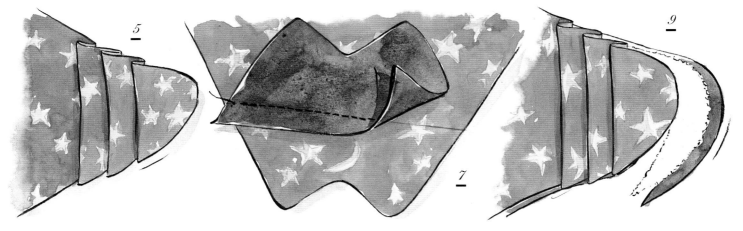

CUTTING OUT AND PREPARATION

1 Using the patterns on page 124, cut out one front, one upper back, one lower back, and four ears from the blue fabric.

2 Cut out the same pieces from the batting.

3 Cut out one front, one upper back, one lower back, one front hoof, and one back hoof from the black lining fabric.

4 On the blue front, mark the pleats and the eye and ear positions.

MAKING THE FRONT

5 To make the narrow pleats in the snout, place the blue front piece right side up. Make an outer fold (bringing wrong sides together) along the right-hand line of each pair of lines. Bring the fold to the left-hand line of the pair.

6 Turn under ½ inch on the straight edge of each black hoof. Place it on the corresponding part of the blue front and mark on the front where the folded edge of the hoof comes to.

7 Unfold the turned-under edge and place the hoof upside-down on the front, with right sides together and matching the fold line to the marked line. Pin and stitch along this line. Turn the hoof to the right side and press. Repeat for the other hoof.

8 Lay the black front lining wrong side up on the work surface, and position the batting front on top of it. Place the blue front on top of the batting, right side up.

9 Matching all edges except the nose edges, pin the three layers together. Trim the batting and black lining so that the nose edges match the pleated blue front. Baste all edges.

MAKING THE BACK

10 Turn under 1 inch along the straight edge of the upper back; press. Turn under and press the same amount again, forming a double hem. (Do not stitch at this stage.) Repeat for the lower back.

11 Trim off 2 inches from the straight edge of the black upper back lining and the batting upper back.

- *Three 17 x 24 inch pieces of lightweight batting*
- *2½ yards medium piping cord*
- *1 yard narrow piping cord*
- *Black embroidery floss*
- *Two oval buttons ½ inch long*
- *Sewing thread to match*

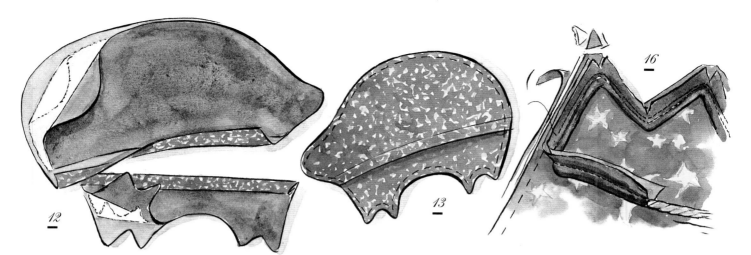

12 Lay the blue upper back wrong side up and position the batting upper back on top of it. Place the black upper back lining on top of the batting, right side up, matching all edges except the straight edge. Unfold the pressed-in hem on the blue fabric and refold it over the batting and black lining. Pin and stitch through all layers along the fold. Baste all raw edges. Repeat for the lower back.

13 Place the upper and lower back with the blue side facing up, and the hemmed edges overlapping by 2 inches. Baste together loosely.

PIPING

14 From the black fabric, make up enough 2 inch wide bias binding to cover 3½ yards of piping cord (page 107). Alternatively, use black readymade bias binding.

15 Use this bias binding to make up about 1 yard of narrow piping and about 2 yards of medium piping (page 107), machine-basting along the seamline. Reserve ½ yard of the medium piping cord for the tail.

16 Pin medium piping to the right (blue) side of the front all around the edges along the seamline, allowing for a ⅝ inch seam. With the zipper foot or piping foot on the machine, stitch through all layers, clipping into the seam allowance on curves so it will lie flat.

EYE AND NOSE

17 Using black embroidery floss, embroider the eye in backstitch, sewing through all three layers. Sew on two buttons for the snout, positioning them vertically.

JOINING FRONT AND BACK

18 With right sides together and raw edges even, pin the front to the backs along the piping line. With the zipper foot or piping foot on the machine, stitch through all layers, taking care to stitch exactly on top of, or just outside, the stitching line for the piping so that it will be within the seam allowance and won't show on the right side. Clip curves, trim off corners, trim seam, remove the basting, and turn right side out through the back opening.

TIP

You will be stitching through no less than eight layers of fabric when joining the front and back: two layers of bias binding, two layers of fabric, and a layer of batting for the front, and the same for the back. It would therefore be advisable to reduce the bulk of the seam allowance after stitching it, to prevent unsightly ridges along the seamlines.

The most obvious way to do this is to trim the batting back to the seamline within the seam

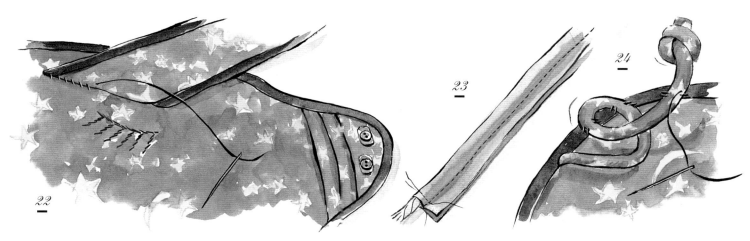

MAKING AND ATTACHING THE EARS

19 Baste batting to the wrong side of all four ear pieces.

20 With right sides together and the zipper foot or piping foot on the machine, stitch narrow piping to each outside ear piece.

21 With right sides together and raw edges even, pin an outside ear piece to an inside ear piece. Stitch all the shaped edges, taking a ⅝ inch seam. Clip the curves. Turn right side out through the unstitched, straight edge; now stitch the straight edge together. Repeat for the other pair of ear pieces.

22 Turn under ⅝ inch along the seamline on the straight edge of each ear; press. Line up the folded edge of each ear with the marked placement line, and hand sew in place.

MAKING AND ATTACHING THE TAIL

23 Cut a ¼ yard strip of bias binding from the blue fabric. With the *wrong* side facing out, wrap it over ½ yard of medium piping. Using a zipper foot or piping foot on the machine, stitch the fabric along the cord. Stitch several stitches securely *through* the piping and fabric at the end nearer the center.

24 Rolling the fabric back along the piping from the unstitched end, turn the binding to the right side. Cut off the excess piping cord, and knot the end. Curl the tail around and hand-sew it to the pig in three places.

allowance. In addition, any seam allowances resulting from lengths of bias binding being joined can be trimmed very close to the stitching within the seam allowance without affecting the strength. Grading, also known as layering, is another way of avoiding ridges. This involves trimming each layer of the seam allowances to a slightly different width. Leave the seam allowance for the blue fabric the widest, for maximum strength.

PRIZE PORKER

This handsome beast has good reason to be pleased with itself, because any child would be thrilled to have such a friendly-looking animal decorating a pillow in the playroom or nursery. The bold, simple shapes and bright colors make it perfect for a child, but it would also look good in a breakfast nook or kitchen. All the pieces are appliquéd onto the pillow cover using simple machine embroidery, so it is both sturdy and washable. Using machine satin stitch and fusible web for the appliqué also makes the process faster than hand appliqué. The simple machine embroidery used on the trees, bushes, grass, and fence provides an ideal opportunity to experiment with different effects.

Finished size 16½ inches square

MATERIALS

- 19 inch square of maroon cotton
- 7 x 5 inches maroon cotton
- 19 x 10½ inches and 19 x 14¼ inches of browny-pink cotton
- 6½ x 5 inch rectangle of browny-pink cotton
- 13 x 9 inch rectangle and 4 inch square of red cotton

PREPARATION AND CUTTING OUT

1 Following the manufacturer's directions, iron the fusible web to all pieces of fabric apart from the maroon front panel and two browny-pink back panels.

2 Using the patterns on page 127, cut out the pig, one of each of the trees and bushes, and four circles from the appropriately colored fabrics.

APPLIQUÉ AND MACHINE EMBROIDERY

3 Zigzag stitch the edges of the maroon front panel and two browny-pink back panels to prevent raveling.

4 Remove the paper backing from the fusible web on the larger red piece. Fuse this to the maroon front panel, leaving a maroon border of 5 inches at the top and bottom and 3 inches at the sides.

5 Remove the paper backing from both pieces of check fabric, and fuse to the front panel too, slightly overlapping the red panel, and leaving a 2¼ inch maroon border all around.

6 Using red thread, machine satin stitch around the edges of the red fabric and check fabric.

7 Peel off the paper backing from the trees, bushes, and circles, and fuse to the front panel, referring to the photograph for positioning.

8 Repeat for the pig, fusing the browny-pink band and ears on top of the light pink.

9 If you have an embroidery foot for your machine, use it as you stitch around the edges of all the shapes, adding detail by "drawing" with the stitches, and using the appropriate colors. Alter the width of the stitches

as necessary. If you don't have an embroidery foot, put the fabric into an embroidery hoop and stitch as above, with *no* foot at all on the machine (see page 109).

10 Changing colors as necessary, fill in the details by stitching over the shapes in the same way.

MAKING THE CUSHION COVER

11 Using a straight-stitch foot on the machine, press and stitch a narrow double hem on one long edge of each of the two back panels.

12 With right sides together and raw edges even, pin the two back panels to the front panel so that the back panels overlap. Stitch all around, taking a ¾ inch seam. Turn right side out. Press.

13 Insert the pillow form through the opening in the back.

- Two 14¼ x 3½ inch rectangles of orange-and-white check cotton
- 13 x 7 inches light pink cotton
- Sewing threads in

orange, pink, maroon, red, and green
- One piece of fusible web for each piece of fabric except the maroon and pink panel pieces

- 18 inch pillow form

BASIC SEWING TECHNIQUES

SEAMS

Most seams are simple flat seams. Place the two pieces of fabric together (normally right sides together) with the raw edges even. Pin along the seamline with the pins at right angles to the seamline. If desired, baste just inside the seamline and remove pins. (This is advisable if you are easing a curved edge onto a straight edge.) Stitch along the seamline specified in the instructions – usually ⅜ to ⅝ inch from the edge – stitching over the pins if your sewing-machine manual recommends it. Work a few stitches in reverse at each end, or tie the threads. Remove the basting if used. Press the seam open unless directed to press it to one side (for example, in patchwork, when seam allowances should be pressed toward the darker fabric).

To sew around a corner, stitch until you reach the seamline of the next edge. Stop the machine with the needle in the fabric, lift the presser foot and pivot the fabric 90° (or less or more, depending upon the corner to be stitched). Lower the presser foot and continue stitching. For very sharp corners on bulky fabrics, work two stitches across the point (1).

On an outer corner, snip off the point within the seam allowance so the corner will be sharp when turned right side out. On an inner corner, snip into the corner within the seam allowance so it will not pucker (2).

To make a curved seam lie flat, clip into the seam allowance on outward curves and snip V-shapes from inward curves (3).

To reduce the bulk of a seam with several layers, "grade," or "layer," the seam allowance by trimming each layer to a different width (4).

For a seam with a selvage edge, clip into the selvage within the seam allowance every 4 inches. This will prevent puckering after cleaning.

A good way to finish the raw edges of a seam is to zigzag stitch them. Use the zigzag presser foot and a short, narrow stitch, zigzagging just in from each raw edge.

BIAS BINDING

To make your own bias binding, you will need to cut bias strips that are four times the desired finished width. Find the true bias of the fabric by first checking that the cut edge is exactly on the crosswise grain, then folding the fabric diagonally so the cut edge is parallel to the selvage. Press the diagonal fold. Mark strips to the correct width parallel to this pressed line, and cut out (5).

To join the strips into a continuous length, pin the ends with right sides together and raw edges even. Stitch across the end taking a ¼ inch seam, press open and cut off the points even with the edge. Join the other ends so that they slant in the same direction (6).

Unless directed otherwise, fold in the edges of the binding so they meet in the center, and press (7).

To bind an edge, unfold one side of the binding and place it along the edge to be bound, with right sides together and raw edges even. Pin and stitch along the crease. Fold the binding to the other side, and either slipstitch or machine stitch it over the previous stitching.

PIPING

To make your own piping, decide the width of the bias binding by wrapping some fabric around your piping cord (which comes in various thicknesses), measuring how much is needed to enclose it and then adding 1 ¼ inches for the seam allowance. Fold the bias binding in half lengthwise, wrong sides together, with the piping cord inside. Using the piping or zipper foot on the machine, pin and stitch fairly close to the cord.

To attach piping, lay it along the seamline of one piece of fabric on the right side, with the cord facing inward and the raw edges even. With the piping or zipper foot on the machine, pin, baste, and stitch just inside the seamline. Lay the other fabric piece on top of the first one, with right sides together and raw edges even, sandwiching the piping between the two layers. Stitch through all four thicknesses along the seamline, as close to the piping cord as possible (8).

If the ends need to be joined, allow 2 inches extra in length for this. Try to position the splice at a seamline or centrally between two edges. To join the ends, leave ⅜ inch unstitched at the first end when attaching the piping, and 2 inches at the other end, then unpick the stitches of the bias binding at those ends. Fold back the fabric. Unravel the ends of the piping cord and trim the strands to different lengths. Overlap the ends by about 1 inch, intertwining the strands. Fold the binding back over the cord, turning under the overlapping end and trimming off any excess fabric if necessary (9).

PLEATS

There are three main types of pleats – box, inverted, and knife – but only knife pleats are used in the projects in this book. Knife pleats all face in the same direction. They are indicated on the pattern by a pleat line (A), which is the outer fold, and a placement line (B). Bringing the two lines together creates the pleat. Sometimes there is a third line (C) halfway between them to indicate the inner fold (10).

ZIPPERS

To insert a zipper, machine baste the opening in the seam where the zipper will go. Press. Open the zipper and place it centrally over the seam, face down on the wrong side. Pin and baste down one side about ⅛ inch away from the teeth, starting and stopping level with the top and bottom of the zipper. Close the zipper and repeat on the other side (11).

Now, from the right side and using the zipper foot, topstitch down the sides just outside the basting and across the ends, stitching as close as possible to the ends without actually going over them (12). Remove the basting, and unpick the machine basting along the seamline.

EMBROIDERY TECHNIQUES

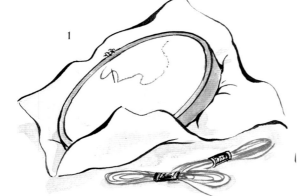

HAND EMBROIDERY

Hand embroidery is often worked on fabric such as gingham or evenweave linen, cotton, or wool. These have a natural grid that is tailormade for charted designs utilizing stitches such as cross-stitch. (However, cross-stitch can also be worked on fabrics with no inherent grid, such as felt, if a piece of "waste canvas," which does have a woven grid, is placed on top. It is embroidered at the same time and then removed thread by thread.) Evenweave fabrics come in various "counts," or numbers of threads per inch, ranging from a coarse 11 to a fine 32.

Cross-stitch is the most common embroidery stitch, but there are countless others, some of which are included in the Stitch Glossary on pages 110–11.

Before beginning to embroider, finish the raw edges of the fabric by zigzag stitching or turning under and hemming the edges.

Unless the piece to be embroidered is very small, it is advisable to place it in a hoop or on a frame so the fabric is stretched taut. To use a hoop, lay the fabric, right side up, over the inner ring, then push the outer ring over it (1). Adjust the fabric and the screw. Always take out the work when you are finished for the day, otherwise the circular creases left in the fabric will be impossible to remove.

Mark the center of the fabric as for page 29, step 1. This point, which corresponds to the center point marked on the chart, is your starting point (2).

In counted-thread embroidery, which is worked from charted designs, each square represents one stitch, and the color or symbol in that square indicates the color. The instructions will specify how many threads each stitch is worked over; for cross-stitch it is generally one or two threads.

Some embroidery threads are stranded and some are not. The instructions will specify which type you use and, if applicable, how many strands (usually one or two for cross-stitch). Do not cut the thread longer than 15–20 inches, or it will become frayed and thin and lose its sheen. The threads are started and fastened off (3), and the colors changed, as for needlepoint (page 29, steps 4 and 9). Also as with needlepoint, you can use either the "sewing" method, in which each stitch is worked in one movement, or the "stabbing" method in which two movements are necessary for each stitch (page 29, step 8).

As you work, be sure to stop often and let the needle dangle from the fabric so the thread will untwist.

When the embroidery is completed, remove the basting thread and press the work by laying it face down on a folded towel on the ironing board and covering with a damp cloth. Press lightly. If it is badly distorted, block it as for needlepoint (page 30, step 12). Do not, however, do this for embroidered clothing. If desired, mount the work as described on page 37, step 7.

MACHINE EMBROIDERY

Machine embroidery can be worked on an ordinary sewing machine using either straight or zigzag stitch. A wide variety of effects is possible, a few of which are shown here (4).

A machine satin stitch – a very close zigzag stitch – is used for machine appliqué. The stitches should be as close together as possible without actually bunching up. Some machines have a special embroidery foot, which has a wide, open "toe" for smoother feeding and better visibility when satin stitching.

Satin stitch and various other forms of decorative stitching can be worked as free embroidery, also known as free-style embroidery or free-motion embroidery. In this the presser foot and feed dog are not used. The fabric is put in an embroidery hoop to keep it taut and moved by hand in the desired direction. The speed at which it is moved determines the stitch length. With a little practice you will probably find it easier to work machine satin stitch using free embroidery.

A wide range of threads can be used, including traditional sewing thread, special machine embroidery thread, and metallic thread. Some attractive effects are possible by using different colors or textures on the top and the bobbin.

The hoop should be about 8–9 inches in diameter and thin enough to clear the needle and the presser bar (which has to be lowered during stitching in order to tension the upper thread). If you are using a hand-embroidery hoop, bind the inner ring with a woven tape such as lampshade-binding tape to prevent the fabric from slipping (5). A spring embroidery hoop will not need binding.

To put the fabric in the hoop, lay it right side up on top of the larger ring, then push the smaller one down into it. (This is the opposite of how it is done in hand embroidery.) Adjust the fabric and the screw so that the fabric is as taut as possible.

To set the machine, refer to your manual, which should say to remove the presser foot, drop or cover the feed dog, set the stitch length to 0, and loosen the upper tension a little.

To start stitching, you need to have the bobbin thread on top of the fabric, so lower the presser bar and turn the hand wheel toward you while holding the upper thread taut, which will bring the bobbin thread up (6). Holding both the top and bobbin flat on the fabric to the left of the needle, secure the threads by taking a few small stitches. Cut off the ends. (Be very careful always to keep your fingers well away from the needle.)

Work first with a stitch width of 0, then as you gain confidence, try zigzagging. Experiment with moving the hoop quickly and slowly to make long and short stitches respectively. Approximately 25 stitches per inch will be about right for intricate designs.

Try turning the hoop in different directions to form small curves and spirals. Experiment with different tensions, both top and bottom. Try "drawing" the outline of a flower, then filling in with close, even lines of free running (straight) stitch.

To move from one area to another, raise the needle to its highest position, lift the presser bar to release the tension, move the hoop, lower the needle and the presser bar, and continue stitching. (The loose thread can be cut off later.)

To finish, make a few small stitches (by moving the hoop slowly) then cut off the ends.

STITCH GLOSSARY

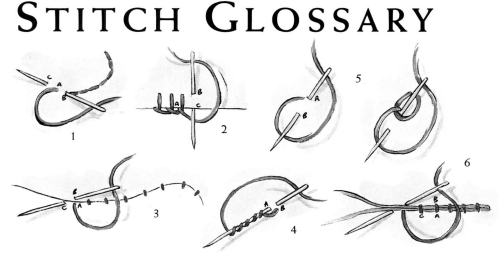

BACKSTITCH (1)

This is used for outlining in embroidery, and in sewing for working a strong seam or finishing off a line of stitching. Working from right to left, bring the needle out at A, insert it at B, and bring it out at C. (Point A should be halfway between B and C.) Repeat, with the old point A becoming point B.

BLANKET STITCH (2)

This is used for decorating edges. Working from left to right, bring the needle out at A, insert it at B, and bring it out at C, which is directly below B and directly to the right of A. Make sure the thread is under the point of the needle as you pull it through. Repeat, with the old point C becoming point A.

BLINDSTITCH (3)

This is used to sew a folded edge to a flat piece, particularly in appliqué. Sometimes called blind hem stitch or overcast stitch, it is similar to slipstitch. Working from right to left, bring the needle through the turned-under edge to the front at A. Insert it directly opposite this in the flat piece at B. Take a small stitch, bringing it out through the turned-under edge at C and pulling it through. Repeat, with the old C becoming A.

BULLION KNOT (4)

This is used for filling or outlining. Bring the needle out at A, insert it at B, and bring it out at A again. With the needle not yet pulled through the fabric, wrap the thread around the point about six times. Carefully pull the needle through the fabric and the twists, then take the thread back toward B to invert the twists. Pull the thread tight, pressing the twists closely together using the needle. Repeat, inserting the needle at B again.

CHAIN STITCH (5)

This is used for outlining. Working vertically, bring the needle out at A. Insert it back at A and bring it out at B, taking the thread under the point of the needle before pulling it through. Repeat, with the old B becoming A.

COUCHING (6)

This is used for outlining and is often the means of securing a very delicate metallic thread (the "laid" thread) to the fabric surface with a less precious, more supple thread (the "working" thread). Bring the desired number of laid threads out at the right. These can be arranged as you work. Bring the working thread out at A, insert it at B, and bring it out at C. Repeat, with the old C becoming A. Continue, making the anchoring stitches the same distance apart. At the end, take the laid threads to the back and fasten off.

CROSS-STITCH (7)

This is used for outlining borders, for lettering, or for filling. It can be worked horizontally (shown here), vertically, or diagonally. The top diagonals should all slope the same way. You can work all the diagonals sloping in one direction, then, at the end of the row, come back and make all the other diagonals, or work one complete stitch at a time.

FEATHER STITCH (8)

This is an embroidery stitch, which is sometimes worked over a seamline in patchwork or appliqué. Working from top to bottom, bring the needle out at A. Insert it at B, and bring it out at C, taking the thread under the point of the needle before pulling through. Repeat in reverse on the other side (inserting it at D and bringing it out at E, again with the thread under the needle point). Continue in the same way. To finish, make a small stitch over the last loop as shown.

FRENCH KNOT (9)

These can be used individually or over a whole area. Bring the needle out and, holding the thread taut with your other hand, wrap the thread around the point of the needle twice (or three or four times if you want French knots on stalks). Still holding the thread taut, insert the needle close to the point at which it originally came out.

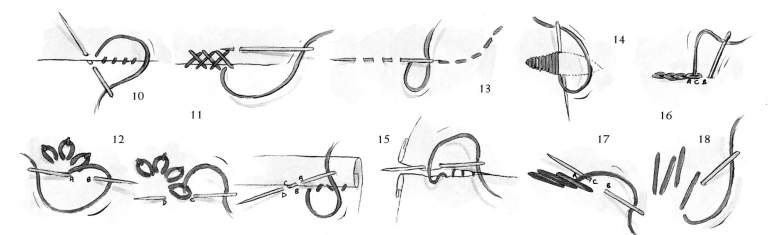

HEMSTITCH (10)

This is used for sewing down folded edges, including hemming lightweight and medium-weight fabrics and securing the edge of seam binding. Take a tiny stitch then bring the needle diagonally up through the hem. Repeat along the entire edge, catching only a thread each time and spacing the stitches evenly and ⅛–¼ inch apart.

HERRINGBONE STITCH (11)

Also known as catchstitch, this is used for embroidering edgings and for sewing heavy or stretchy fabrics together. Working from left to right, take small stitches from right to left, first at the top (in the fold of the upper layer if you are sewing rather than embroidering) then at the bottom (in the lower layer of fabric if sewing).

LAZY DAISY STITCH (12)

This is a detached chain stitch. Groups of these stitches are often arranged in circles to look like flowers. Bring the needle out at A, then insert it at A again, and bring it out at B, taking the thread under the point of the needle before pulling it through. Insert it at C and bring it out at D, ready to start the new stitch, in which the old D becomes the new A.

RUNNING STITCH (13)

This is the easiest stitch for outlining in embroidery. It is also the most basic of the sewing stitches, used for seams, gathering, and many other purposes. A running stitch that is longer on the right side than on the wrong side is used for basting. Pick up several stitches before pulling the needle through, and keep the stitches even.

SATIN STITCH (14)

This is a filling stitch. Working from left to right, make long, straight lines next to each other and close together.

SLIPSTITCH (15)

This may be used to sew a folded edge to a flat piece of fabric invisibly. Also known as slip hemming when used in this way, it is worked from right to left. Insert the needle at A, and take a small stitch, sliding the needle inside the fold for about ¼ inch. Bring it out of the fold at B, then insert it into the other piece of fabric at C, either directly opposite or about ¹⁄₁₆ inch farther on. Catch one or two threads and bring it out at D, pulling the thread through. Now repeat the stitch, inserting the needle either directly opposite D. or ¹⁄₁₆ inch farther on. You can also use slipstitch to sew two folded edges together invisibly. Work it in the same way, but slide the needle through both folds, not just one.

SPLIT STITCH (16)

This is used principally for outlining. Working from left to right, bring the needle out at A, insert it at B, and bring it out at C, splitting the thread. Repeat, with the old C becoming A.

STEM STITCH (17)

This is mainly for outlining, and for embroidering stems. Working from left to right, bring the needle out at A, insert it at B, then bring it up again at C, which should be halfway between A and B. Repeat, with the old C becoming point A. The needle coming out at the new C shares the hole with the thread that was inserted when it was the old B.

STRAIGHT STITCH (18)

This is used to embroider straight lines in a design. It is worked like a single line of satin stitch.

ENLARGING AND TRANSFERRING DESIGNS

ENLARGING THE DESIGN

If the design needs to be enlarged, you can do this on a photocopier; for example, to make each dimension twice as large, you would set the copier for 200 per cent. Alternatively, you can draw a grid of squares on the design and then copy each square onto a grid of larger squares; ½ inch squares, for instance, could be copied onto 1 inch squares if you wanted the dimensions to be twice as large.

TRANSFERRING THE DESIGN

There are various ways of transferring a design to fabric, cardboard, or the backing paper of fusible web. Start by either tracing it from the book onto tracing paper (if it is the correct size) or enlarging it. Then do one of the following:

• Place dressmaker's carbon paper between the paper and the fabric and then draw over it. (Test first to make sure it will wash out.) Be careful not to smudge it.

• Dot the outline on the back of the tracing with a transfer pencil and then iron this onto the fabric following the manufacturer's directions. (Make sure beforehand that it will wash out.)

• Shade the back of the traced design with a soft pencil, then place the tracing on the fabric or cardboard, pencil side down, and draw around the design with a ballpoint pen.

• Cut out the outline of the design and . draw around it using a fadeaway pen.

• Trace the design straight onto a fine fabric or stencil card by taping both to a window (or laying it on a light box or on a glass coffee table with a lamp underneath).

• If you are transferring the design onto fabric, trace it first onto tissue paper, then work running stitches all around the outline through both fabric and tissue paper. Carefully tear away the tissue paper.

Remember that methods which involve drawing or to the back of something will come out the reverse (mirror) image of the original design. This happens, for instance, if you transfer the design to the backing paper of fusible web (which is why the patterns in this book that are used with fusible web are in reverse).

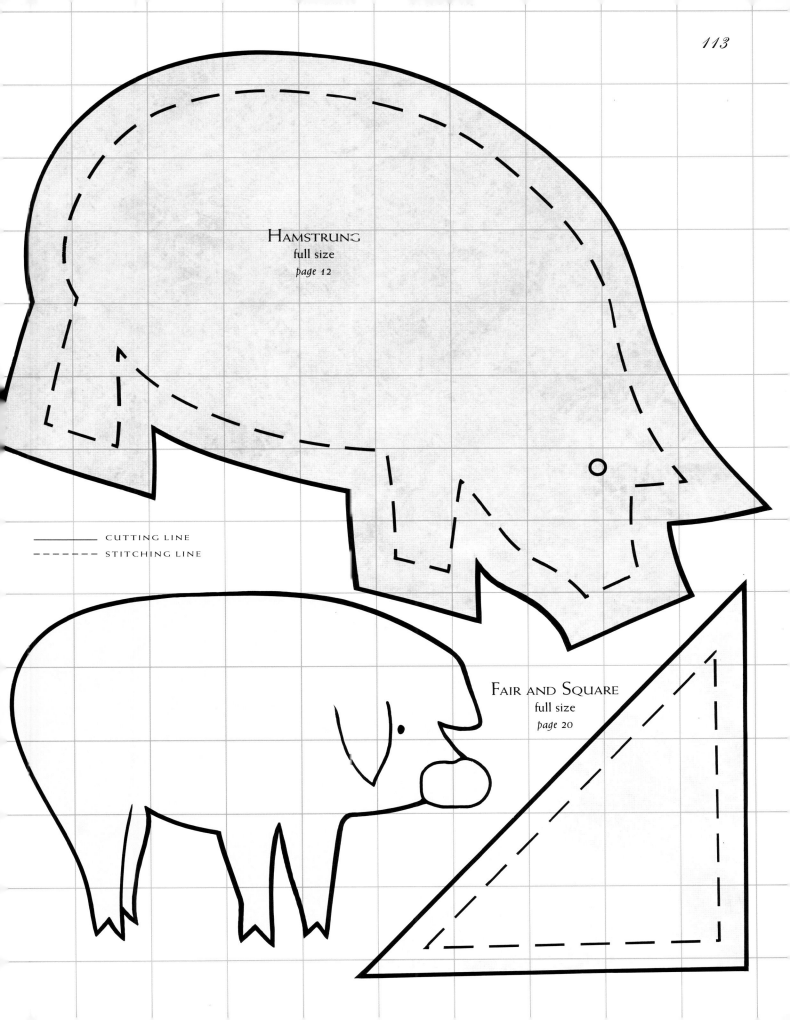

HAMSTRUNG
full size
page 12

CUTTING LINE
STITCHING LINE

FAIR AND SQUARE
full size
page 20

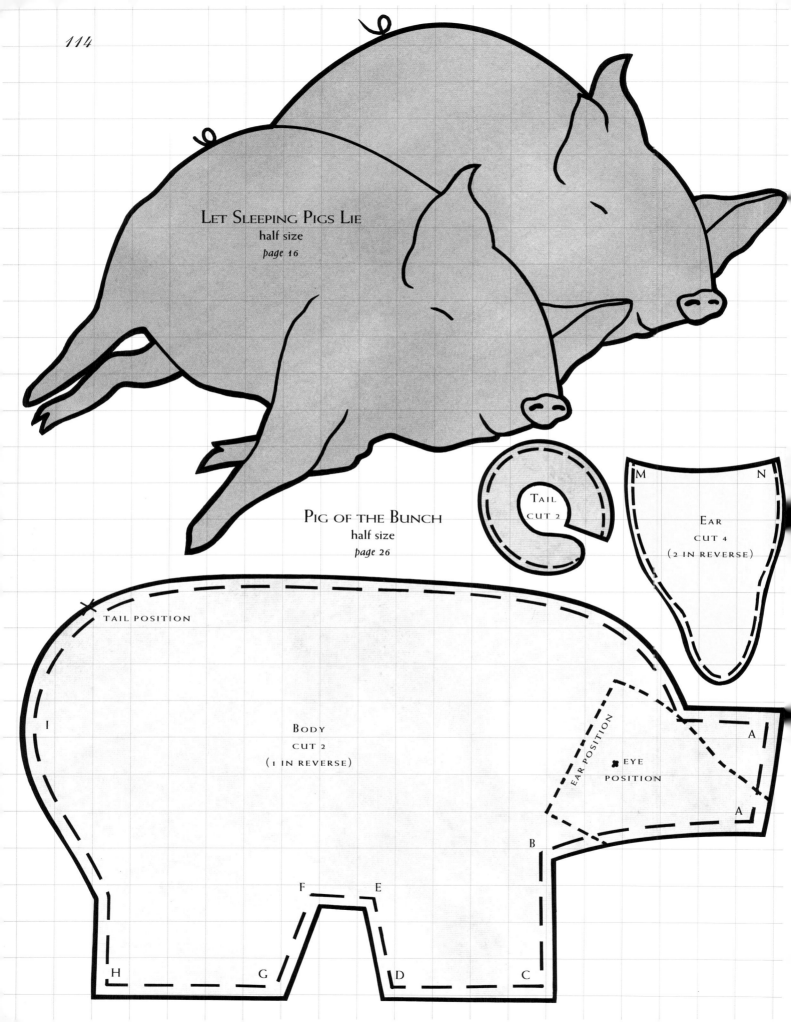

LET SLEEPING PIGS LIE
half size
page 16

PIG OF THE BUNCH
half size
page 26

TAIL
CUT 2

M   N

EAR
CUT 4
(2 IN REVERSE)

TAIL POSITION

I

BODY
CUT 2
(1 IN REVERSE)

EAR POSITION

EYE
POSITION

A

A

B

F   E

H   G   D   C

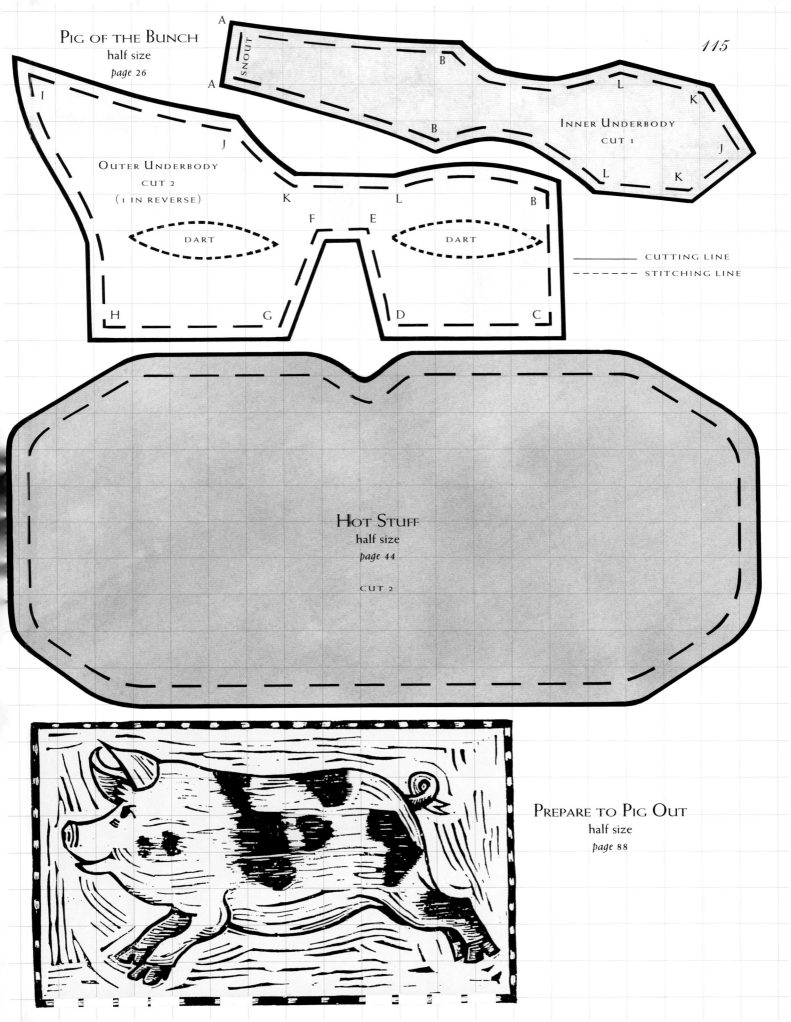

Pig of the Bunch
half size
page 26

SNOUT

A
A
B
B

Inner Underbody
CUT 1

L
K
L
K
J

Outer Underbody
CUT 2
(1 IN REVERSE)

I
J

K
L
B

F
E

DART
DART

H
G
D
C

——— CUTTING LINE
- - - - STITCHING LINE

Hot Stuff
half size
page 44

CUT 2

Prepare to Pig Out
half size
page 88

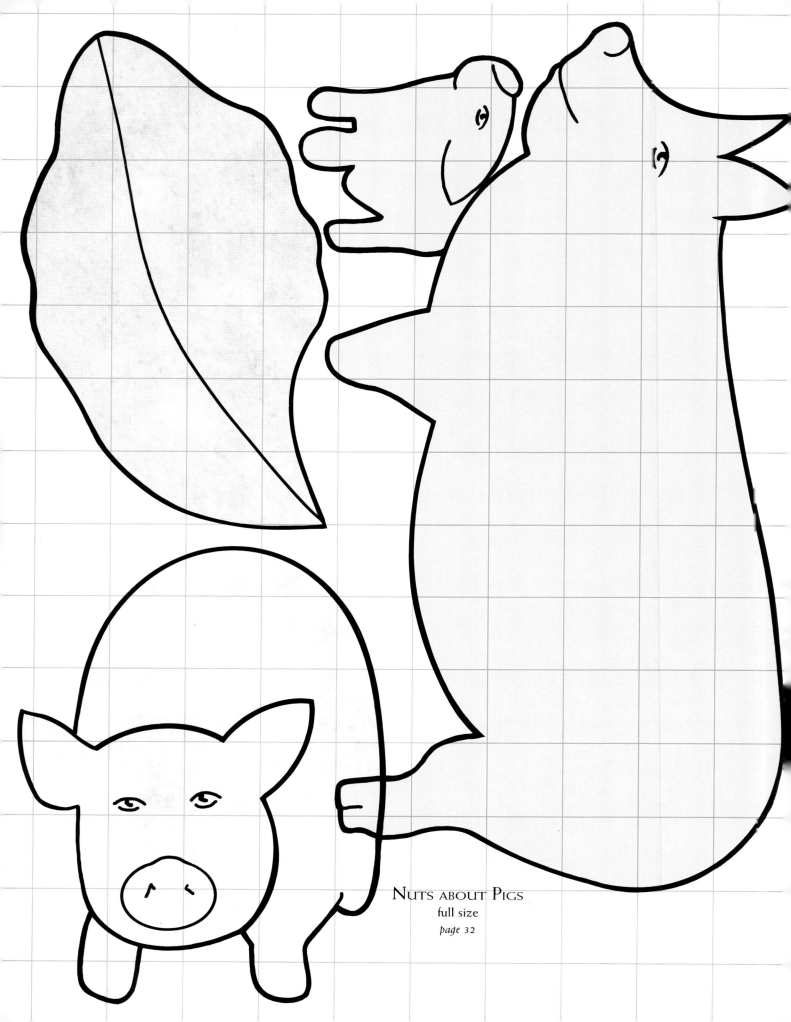

Nuts about Pigs
full size
page 32

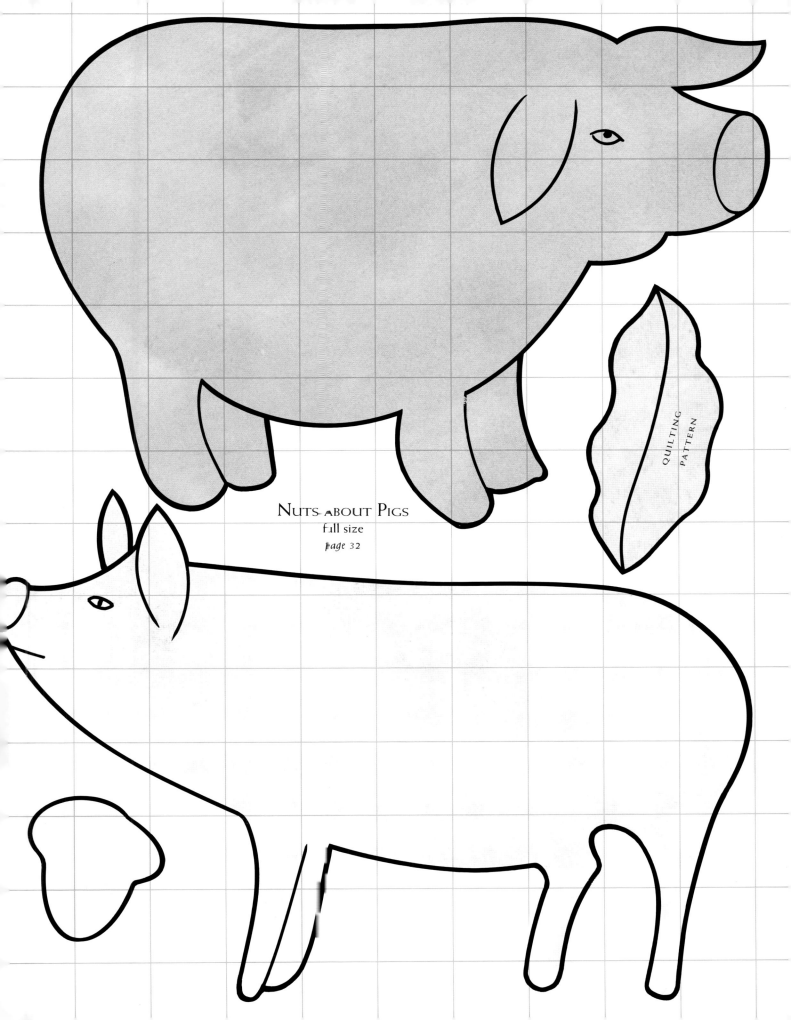

NUTS ABOUT PIGS
full size
page 32

QUILTING PATTERN

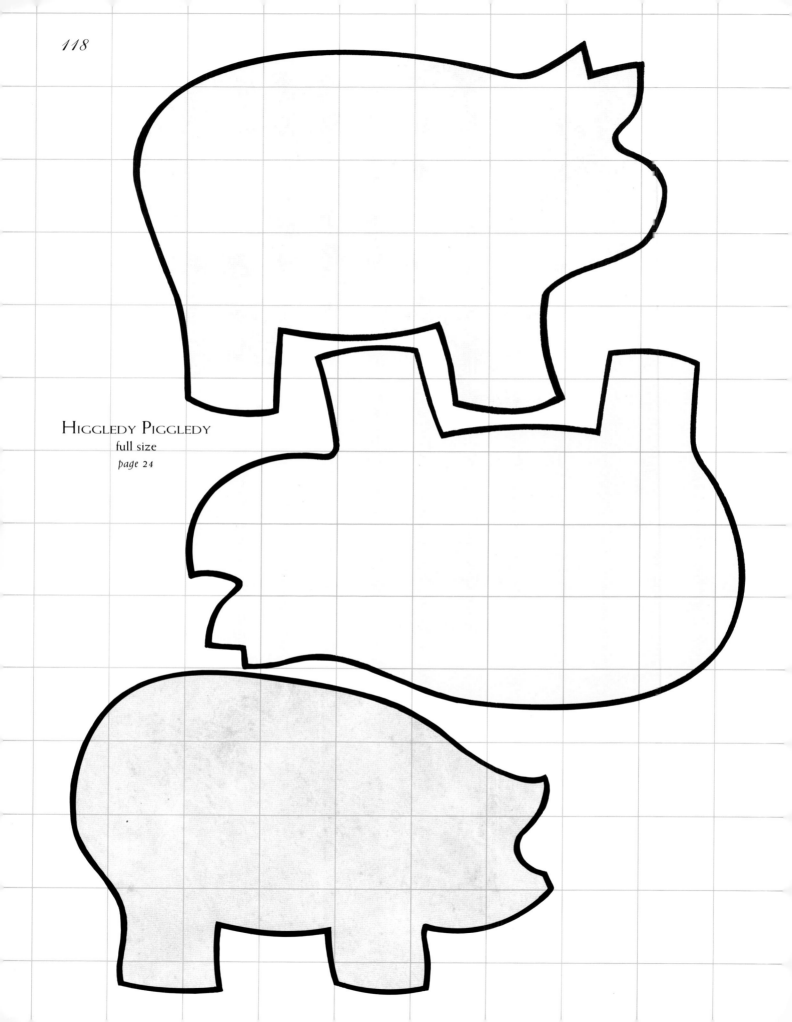

HIGGLEDY PIGGLEDY
full size
page 24

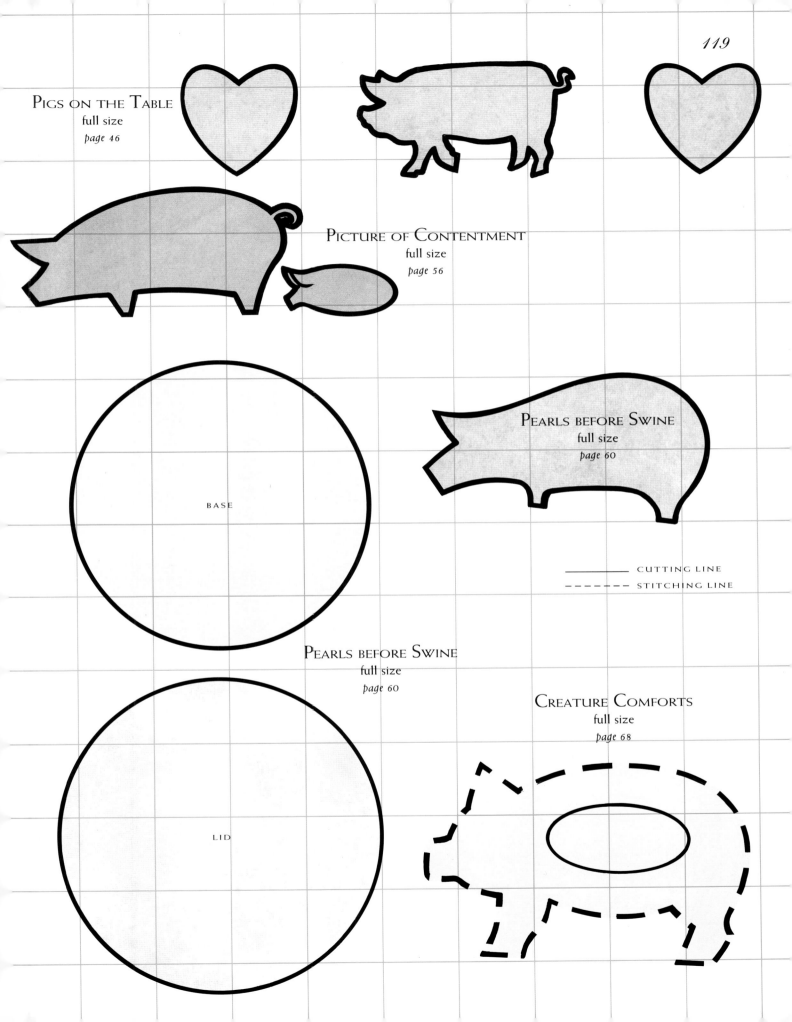

PIGS ON THE TABLE
full size
page 46

PICTURE OF CONTENTMENT
full size
page 56

BASE

PEARLS BEFORE SWINE
full size
page 60

CUTTING LINE
STITCHING LINE

PEARLS BEFORE SWINE
full size
page 60

LID

CREATURE COMFORTS
full size
page 68

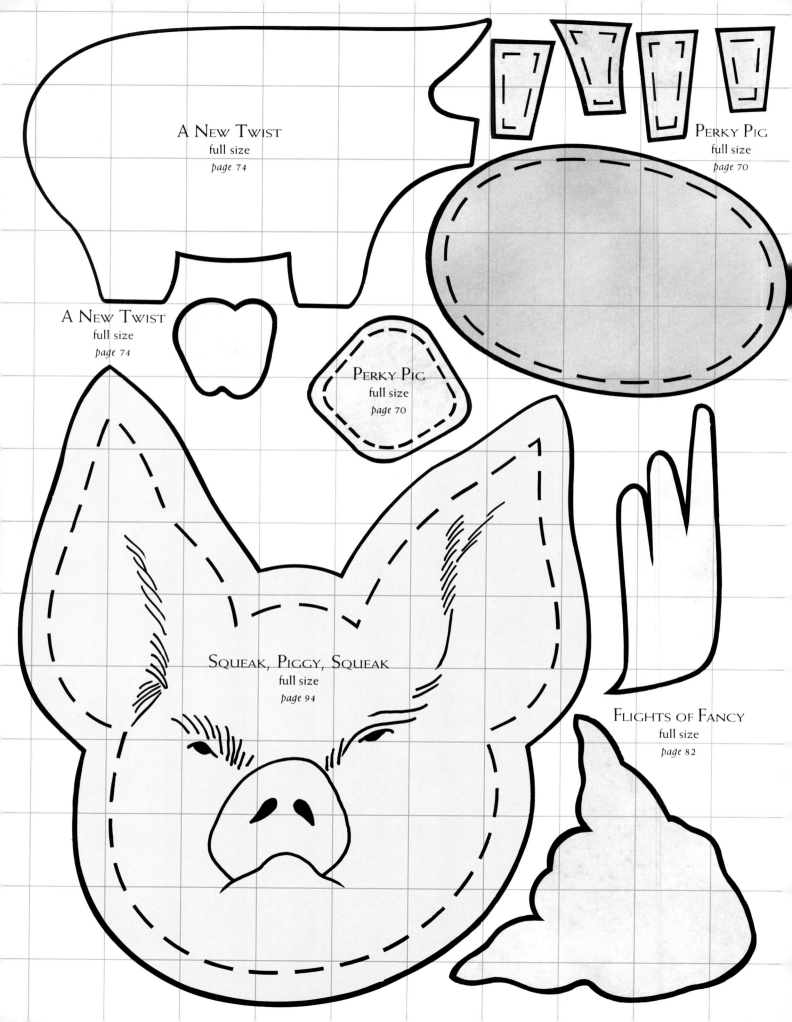

A New Twist
full size
page 74

Perky Pig
full size
page 70

A New Twist
full size
page 74

Perky Pig
full size
page 70

Squeak, Piggy, Squeak
full size
page 94

Flights of Fancy
full size
page 82

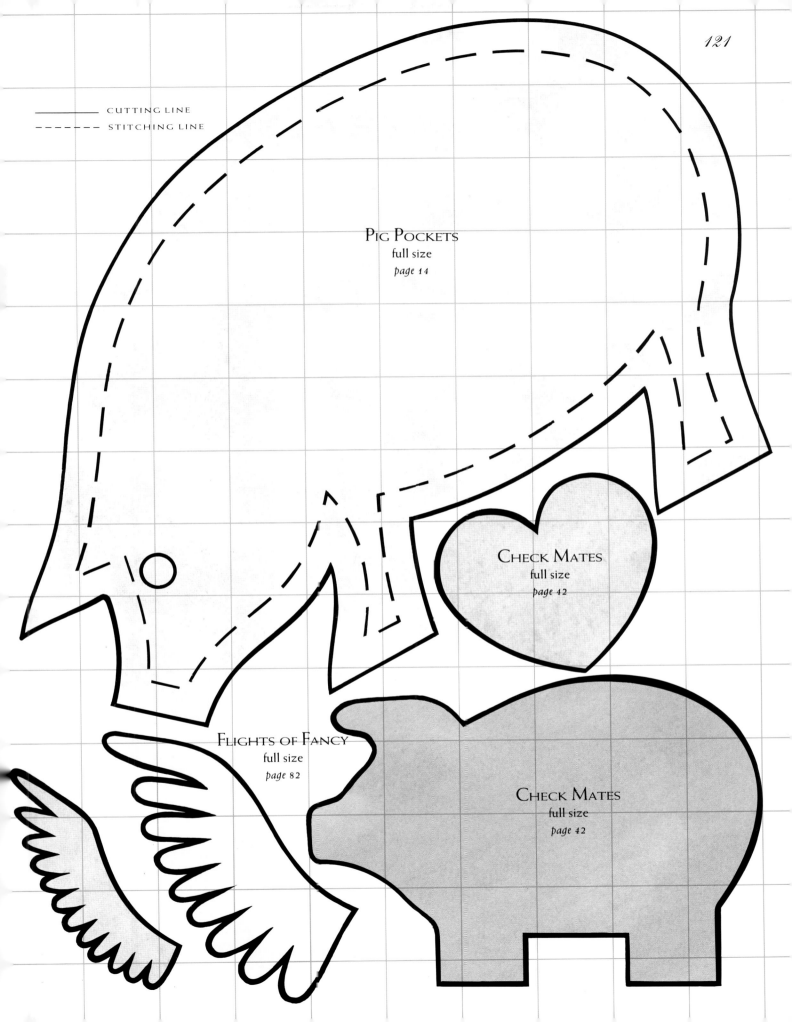

CUTTING LINE

STITCHING LINE

PIG POCKETS
full size
page 14

CHECK MATES
full size
page 42

FLIGHTS OF FANCY
full size
page 82

CHECK MATES
full size
page 42

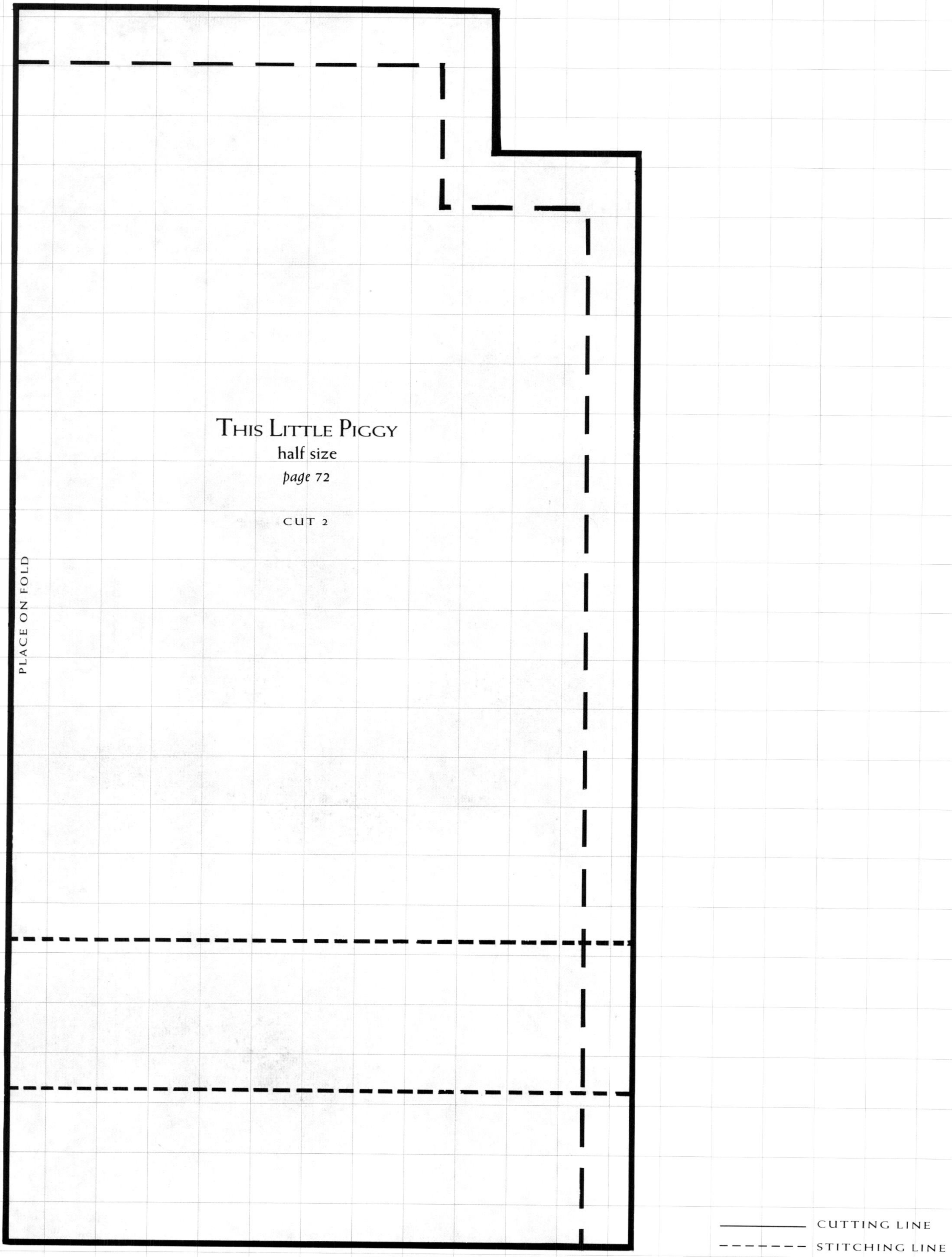

THIS LITTLE PIGGY
half size
page 72

CUT 2

PLACE ON FOLD

CUTTING LINE
STITCHING LINE

FROM HEAD TO TAIL
half size
page 96

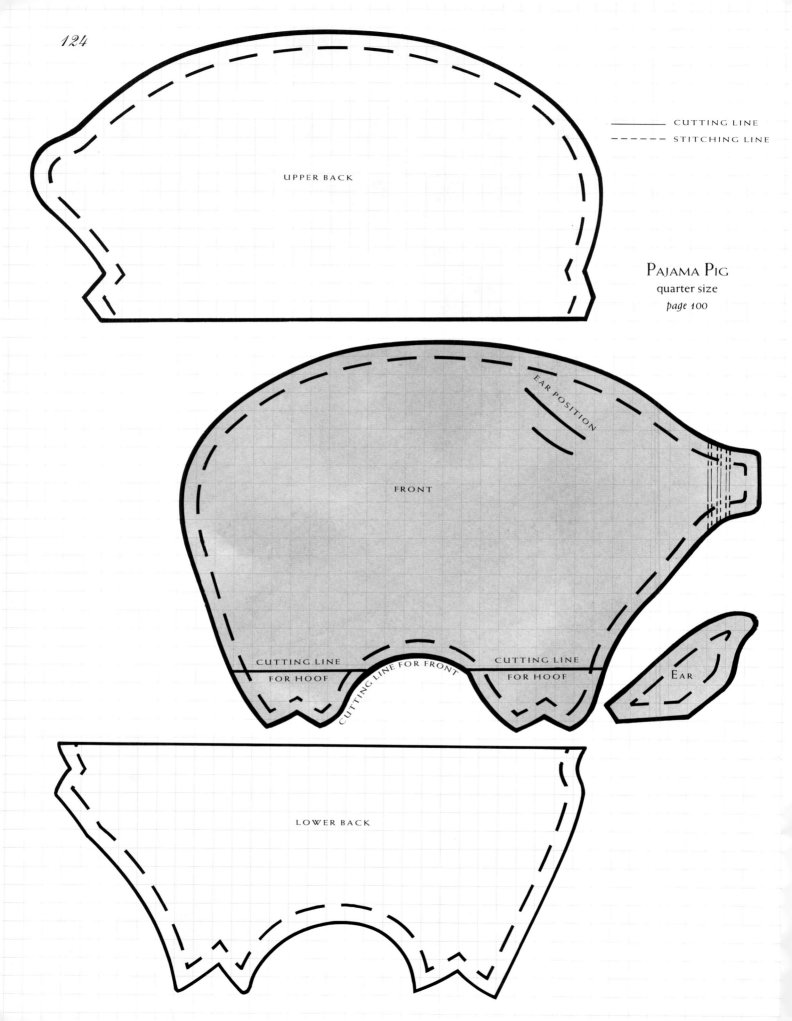

124

CUTTING LINE
STITCHING LINE

UPPER BACK

PAJAMA PIG
quarter size
page 100

FRONT

EAR POSITION

EAR

CUTTING LINE
FOR HOOF

CUTTING LINE FOR FRONT

CUTTING LINE
FOR HOOF

LOWER BACK

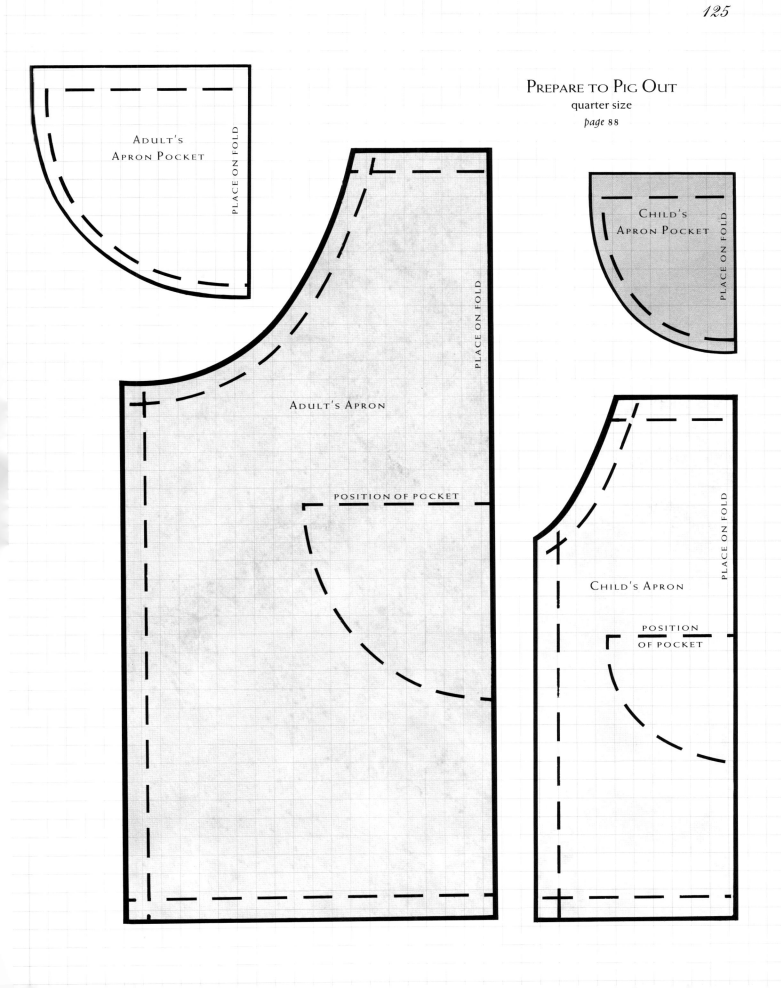

PREPARE TO PIG OUT
quarter size
page 88

ADULT'S
APRON POCKET

PLACE ON FOLD

CHILD'S
APRON POCKET

PLACE ON FOLD

ADULT'S APRON

PLACE ON FOLD

POSITION OF POCKET

CHILD'S APRON

PLACE ON FOLD

POSITION
OF POCKET

126

A

E

C

EAR POSITION

D

F

X
EYE POSITION

G

SNOUT
CUT 2
IN VELVET

BODY BACK
CUT 2
(1 IN REVERSE)

BODY FRONT
CUT 2
(1 IN REVERSE)

J

I

ARM POSITION

ARM
CUT 4

J

I

I

K

B

K

H

K

SHOWING THE DOOR
half size
page 50

C

D

EAR
CUT 4 IN VELVET
(2 IN REVERSE)

UP FRONT
half size
page 86

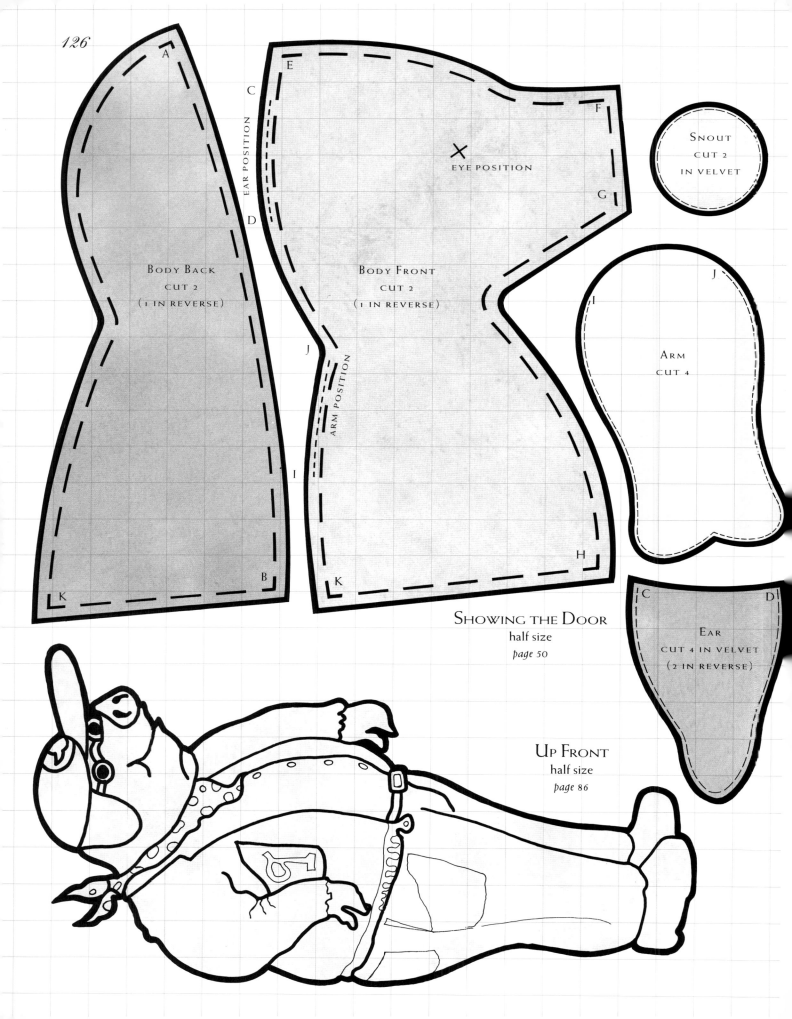

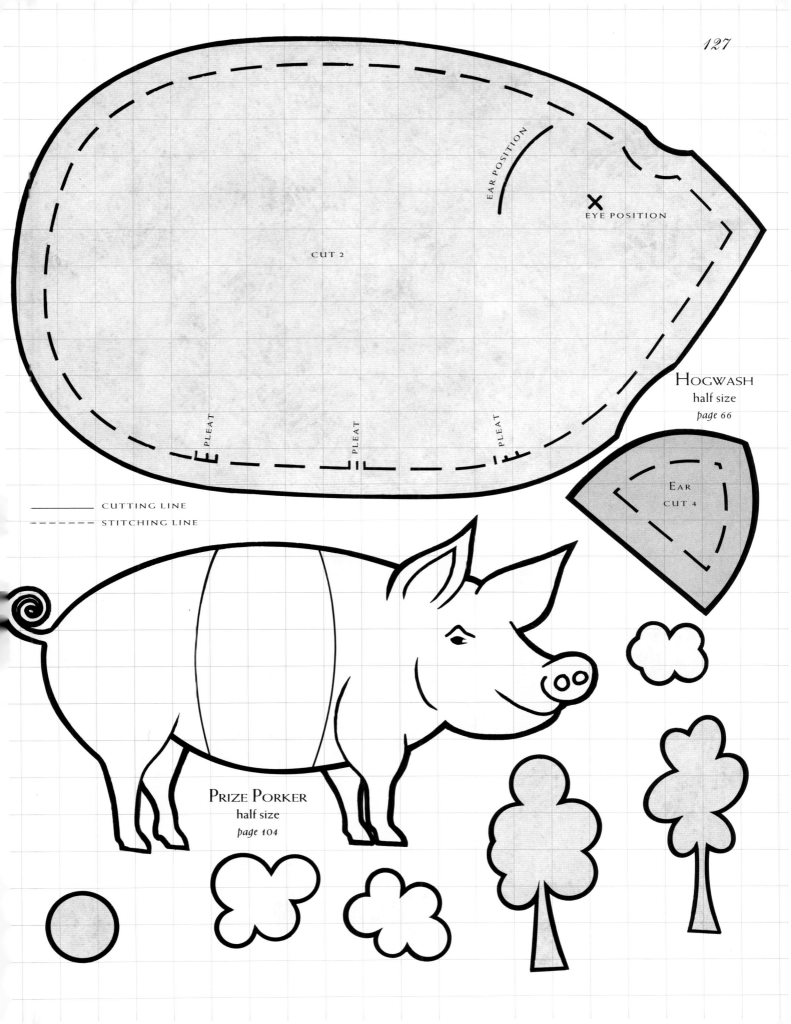

EAR POSITION

✕
EYE POSITION

CUT 2

PLEAT

PLEAT

PLEAT

HOGWASH
half size
page 66

EAR
CUT 4

——— CUTTING LINE
- - - - STITCHING LINE

PRIZE PORKER
half size
page 104

Index

CREDITS

Quarto would like to thank the following craftspeople who contributed projects to the book:

96–9 Louise Bell, The Old Fire Station, 3 Shepherd Street, St. Leonards, East Sussex TN38 0ET
74–7, 100–3 Janis Bullis, Central Valley, NY10917
56–9, 60–3 Irene Hardwick, 69 Rougham Green, Bury St Edmunds, Suffolk IP30 9JP
46–9 Emma Hardy
82–3 Karen Holt
26–7, 50–1, 94–5 Joyce Luckin, Greenfinches, Hillside Walk, Storrington, Pulborough, West Sussex RH20 3HL
36–9, 78–81, 92–3 Hilary Mackin
32–5 Natalia Manley, 133 Crisp Rd, Henley-on-Thames, Oxon RG9 2EU
28–31, 70–1 Elizabeth McDonald Designs, P.O. Box 2828, London NW6 2LZ
104–5 Lucy Merriman, 2/4 Rufus Street, Old Street, London N1 6PE
16–19, 20–3, 52–5 Helen Milosavljevich
42–3, 44–5, 66–7, 68–9, 72–3 Hilary More
86–7 Julia Richardson
88–91 Susanna Rose, Unit 2B Leroy House, 436 Essex Rd, London N1 3QP
12–13, 14–15 Lesley Tonge, 20 Wellfield Ave, London N10 2EA
24–5 Melanie Williams, Bronllys Castle, Bronllys, Powys, Wales LD3 0HL

Quarto would like to thank the following for providing photographs and for permission to reproduce copyright material:
1 Guido Rossi/Image Bank; 2 Nick Gurgul/Ace Photo Agency; 3 (in frame) Sylvia Cordaiy Photo Library; 5 Colin Molineaux/Image Bank; 6 below left Lynn M. Stone/Image Bank; 6 right Bruno Zarri/Ace Photo Agency; 8 center Nick Gurgul/Ace Photo Agency; 9 above Tony Larkin/Rex Features; 9 center Guido Rossi/Image Bank; 10 Andy Sacks/Tony Stone Images; 40 Art Wolfe/Tony Stone Images; 64 Kevin Horan/Tony Stone Images; 84 Andy Sacks/Tony Stone Images. All other photographs are the copyright of Quarto Publishing.